I0168987

The Sober Experience

Samantha Roome

THE SOBER EXPERIENCE

First published in 2025

Copyright © Samantha Roome 2025

The moral rights of the author have been asserted.

All rights reserved. No part of this publication may be reproduced, stored in a retrieval system or transmitted in any form or by any means, electronic, mechanical, photocopying, audio recording or otherwise without the prior permission of the author.

ISBN paperback 978-1-0683234-0-9
ISBN ebook 978-1-0683234-1-6

IMPORTANT NOTE TO READERS

This book has been written and published for informational and educational purposes only.

Any use of information in this book is at the readers' discretion and risk. The author cannot be held responsible for any loss, claim or damage arising out of the use or misuse of the suggestions made. No liability is assumed by the author and the reader is entirely responsible for his or her own actions.

Contents

Preface   V

1. Introducing The Sober Experience   1

2. My story   13

3. Part I   35
   Destination

4. Part II   53
   Knowledge

5. Part III   78
   Awareness

6. Lesson 1   79
   Understanding the link between alcohol and your brain

7. Lesson 2   89
   How to change your mindset around alcohol

8. Part IV   104
   Positivity

9. Lesson 3   105
   Building a story around the statement

10. Lesson 4   109
    Creating a positive picture of a life without alcohol

11.	CHECKPOINT	115
12.	Part V	118
	Tools	
13.	Lesson 5	119
	Recognising and overcoming triggers and cravings	
14.	Lesson 6	131
	Overcoming ambivalence	
15.	Lesson 7	137
	It's not a slip up, it's a learning experience	
16.	CHECKPOINT	142
17.	Part VI	144
	Continuing the adventure	
18.	Lesson 8	145
	The Four Energies	
19.	Lesson 9	151
	Enjoying the freedom of control	
20.	Lesson 10	157
	Climb your own mountain	
21.	CHECKPOINT	162
22.	References	168
23.	APPENDIX I	171
	Alcohol information	
24.	APPENDIX II	179
	Additional Information on my website	
25.	More from the author	180

Preface

"It is my mission to normalise the conversation around alcohol. Everyone has the right to feel supported if they need it."

Have you ever experienced a friendship that was a little one sided? A drain on your energy levels, seemingly fun at times but in reality, much more of a burden than a blessing. Well, when I really thought about it, weighing up thousands of instances along that spectrum of emotions, I finally concluded that this is how it was with me and alcohol and so we decided to part company....

Introducing The Sober Experience

Hello, my name is Sam, and I am a Sober Coach and passionate advocate of having real conversations around alcohol. This book introduces you to The Sober Experience, what it might look like and how to get there. If alcohol has been taking up too much space in your life, then I liken the Sober Experience to waving a magic wand, and who wouldn't want to see how that turns out?

What this book can offer you

This book draws from thirty years of my own experience living with what I thought was a "normal" drinking habit, my own sober story, my childhood lost to my parents' alcoholism, a career path change to qualifying as a Sober Coach, voluntary work in the sober space and four years of research into different theories and philosophies all combining to form this uniquely positive invitation to The Sober Experience.

What this book will cover.

- **Important background information about the effect alcohol has on your mind and body.**

- **Well regarded theories that complement and support The**

Sober Experience

- **Ten Lessons that I have developed through a combination of research, working with clients and my own experience. These lessons are the key to understanding and changing your relationship with alcohol. They comprise insights into every aspect of moving on from an unwanted drinking habit, together with Actions and Journal prompts to help you integrate them into your everyday life - and reap the positive effects.**

If you are considering a life without alcohol or taking a break from alcohol, if you are curious about any kind of alcohol change, if you are simply curious about the impact alcohol has on your mind and brain - then this book is written for you.

Alternatively, if you want to support an individual in your life who is struggling with alcohol – this book will give you more of an understanding of ways to support change.

I'm aware that the very word 'sobriety' can make people feel uncomfortable. Does exploring sobriety mean you'll become serious and boring? Have less fun at parties. Not be invited to parties! Find it hard to unwind after work? Face a challenging day of parenting without 'Mummy/daddy wine' to look forward to?

I too worried about what saying 'Goodbye to alcohol' might be like. But I discovered that what it really felt like was "where had my life been hiding all that time?!" My life was never the same again. It was completely transformed for the better.

It's my mission to normalise the conversation around alcohol, so I've written this book for everyone. But it can be particularly worthwhile for you if

-

- You feel like drinking is more of a burden than a pleasure.

- You're aware that your emotions are driven by drinking, and that you use alcohol as a coping mechanism for stress.

- You've become fed up with the lethargy, brain fog and 'hangxiety' that follows drinking.

- You have a nagging feeling that drinking isn't good for you, despite it being within 'normal' limits.

- You've tried other sober challenges but returned to your regular drinking levels afterwards.

- You want to discover the parts of yourself and your life that alcohol might have been masking, discover whether exploring sobriety will give you the energy and insight you need to create something different.

Experiencing a period without alcohol is increasingly popular, free, there are no side effects, and it can be like rocket fuel for your life but the barrier to giving it a try can often be the fear of not succeeding, the fear of what it actually looks like and the confusion as to whether you are really a valid candidate. Often the messaging around alcohol change is very biased. It contains blame, weakness, guilt, gloom. I challenge all of that:

Where you may have heard weakness, I say addictive substance. How can consuming a legal and addictive substance to excess be a weakness?

Where you may believe you will be permanently tarnished with a label that says "I can't drink" I offer you a life where not drinking might become your **choice.**

Where you experience fear or uncertainty, I provide reassurance.

My approach is a supportive and positive one and addresses all of those fears and misconceptions. If you are stuck in a drinking habit, you already know it doesn't feel good, so focusing on the negative won't push you forward as it keeps your mind stuck back where you don't want to be. But change the focus to the present and you can get to the place where alcohol isn't in control, and that's where the good stuff happens. In this book I will give you the tools and confidence to switch your mind into sober mode.

There are programs for changing your relationship with alcohol which require you to stop drinking completely at the start and maintain your sobriety throughout. The Sober Experience doesn't take that approach. Instead, it's more about gently understanding and exploring your relationship with alcohol at your own pace. The intention is that as your knowledge builds your alcohol consumption will drop, and that you'll reach a point when it no longer becomes the focus of your life.

We don't use labels

Society loves labels. Part of the reason I believe people don't embark on changing their relationship with alcohol is because they can't find a label to suit them and so without that label, didn't consider it was something that needed addressing. If you are unfit, you might join a class or enlist a personal trainer. If you are unhealthy you might chat to a nutritionist. If you need support for an exam, you might engage a tutor. But what label do you give yourself where alcohol is concerned? You habit might not feel serious enough for the label of "alcoholic" or you might just be uncomfortable with that term but you can't find another label that fits. Well, I am here to tell you you don't need a label, you just need to follow an idea - an idea that alcohol might be masking some of your life. You don't need a label to make a change.

The Sober Experience

It is exactly as it says - giving yourself the opportunity to experience sobriety, possibly for the first time in your adult life. I'd like you to approach this experience as you would a journey:

Destination: we take a look at where we are going, what it looks like, feels like and what signals might have led us to embark on this journey.

Packing: we take on board the theories that support the experience – building the knowledge.

Departure: we start the lessons, building from awareness with the mind and brain, positivity in the picture we are creating, and tools to support the experience.

Continuing the adventure: we finish with the next chapter of your life and what it might look like.

It is this whole process, the whole **experience,** which helps to support the mind shift and create a life map where alcohol just isn't necessary or desired.

Removing alcohol gives you permission to do life differently. It is truly the best thing I have ever done for my life, and I have met thousands of people through my coaching and sober groups who would agree. Wouldn't you like to explore what it can do for you?

Why did I write a book?

There is so much power in a book, especially where a habit is concerned, so I have packaged up my thoughts, my understandings and interpretations and my unique path to The Sober Experience into this book.

There is power in reading because the picture of sobriety is often seen as bleak, the unwanted outcome for the unlucky few who couldn't control their drinking, who were too weak to moderate. It is perceived as a cross that some people have to bear but no one would ever actively choose it as a lifestyle choice! I wanted to paint the real picture, so I challenge all of that here.

The path to alcohol change is very often not a clear cut one so the book is there for as long as you need it. A book might feel less daunting than first engaging with coaching or a sober group (although I highly recommend finding a sober group as the connection is proven to really boost going alcohol free). I want you to be able to skip to a chapter or specific page and re-read it when you need to. This may not be your first rodeo. A book can be carried around with you when you are triggered. It can become your portable support tool for as long as you need it.

Initial questions

How do I approach this? Good point. You have bought, borrowed, or been gifted this book. Do you immediately try to stop drinking and feel like you are white knuckling it? Do you lock yourself in a room and read the whole book in one sitting and, fingers crossed, by the end you will be fixed. I hate to say it, because I am one of those people who favours one clear answer over a number of options, but "see how you feel." The process that I share with you might land right away or you might need time and repetition to absorb it. If you do start right now with removing the alcohol you are welcome to skip to Lesson 5 to support you through the first few days.

Is reading this book enough? No. The basis of the book is **change**. As you will learn in Lesson 3 change will involve bringing other influences on board whether that be sober podcasts, other sober stories that you might relate to, new learning, new activities, more moving less sitting. You will need to take action to make any change stick so just reading this book won't be enough. This book will give you learning and a process to follow, but you will need to bring other elements into that process.

How long will it take to change my relationship with alcohol? As with the above, it really depends how fully you absorb what you are reading and if you are able to engage with the exercises. As you will quickly learn along the way, the mind is extremely powerful, and this will trip you up if you let it. It also depends on external factors that might be impacting you right now. If there are other elements negatively affecting your life you might not have the head space to focus 100%. But again, that is why I wrote the book. You can re-read it when you feel stronger.

I don't want to stop entirely. We call this moderation. I have written a section on this topic in Part I. I can't answer this one for you, but I can say as you progress through this experience, moderation stops being the end goal. So don't worry at this moment what outcome you are looking for. Just focus on now.

Will I ever get to a point where I don't crave a drink? – Lesson 5 is all about cravings as they come in different forms. But in a nutshell, the physical cravings can last up to 10 days as the body physically withdraws from alcohol and the emotional and psychological cravings start to fade over time as we do the work on the mind. Yes, it is possible to no longer crave a drink when you stop seeing alcohol as a comfort and when you change the routines and patterns so the habit fades.

When will I start to feel fantastic? Feeling amazing seems to be a common expected outcome amongst those trying sobriety. But this result will depend on what effort you put into this. You should start to notice improved sleep, skin, energy, and mental clarity after 7-10 days as the alcohol leaves your system. That alone was a game changer for me. But in terms of further changes, if you use that energy and clarity to introduce activities that will improve your wellbeing, then absolutely you will start to feel fantastic over the coming months. The more you put in, the bigger the impact. You might be looking out for some huge obvious changes, and they might not come right away as they will require more of a lifestyle shift, but one which you will now have the energy to start!

A sobering thought

It's quite possible with all of our social conditioning that planting the word sober right there, right at the start, is already making you feel uncomfortable, a sense of foreboding is setting in. So, let's start with a few definitions about sober folk.

> **Someone who is sober is not drunk**
> **Someone who is sober is serious and thinks a lot**

Ah yes, I see the problem with the word sobriety. We seem to have amalgamated the two definitions. The sober non-drinking person is also serious. It just sounds boring! But this book is here to tell you sobriety is anything but. Did you notice the other word in my book title? "Experience!" I want you to focus on this word and see what happens. This Sober Experience is here for anyone who is remotely curious about alcohol change. It isn't time bound as I just want you to try it and see how you feel.

Life can be so hectic, and alcohol seems to be the de-stress solution. Life can feel so empty, and alcohol fills the void, numbs the loneliness. Life can feel unfair, and alcohol deadens the memories. One day we realise we forgot how to do it all without the alcohol. Then deep down we might start to wonder, is it really helping? Is alcohol really a **solution?** Deep down we know that, as a response to life, this isn't sustainable. But somewhere along the line it can become the only automatic response to life for some of us.

Alcohol is a highly addictive drug and that is the bottom line, so it should come as no surprise that for many people it becomes an unwanted intruder into daily life. But I ask you,

"If alcohol is the answer, what exactly was the question?"

That there is the answer to change. In our heads it has become this incredibly powerful influence in our lives. We think life would be impossible without it. We avoid removing it because we have told ourselves it won't be easy. With each attempt or consideration, we eventually convince ourselves we don't really need to stop. We are willing to battle through the difficult parts of the habit, all the while refusing to acknowledge them, just to keep the habit going.

Invisible hooks

But why? How did we get to this point? It's all about the story we have been telling ourselves, the narrative that has been driving our life. It's how we have built alcohol up in our head. Your story isn't my story of course. There will be plenty of overlap thanks to those external influences that push alcohol into every phase of life, but your story will have unique attributes that explain why **you** needed to drink. Your story contains the invisible hooks you have linked to alcohol: the laughter on all of those nights out - the hook is that the memory has told you that alcohol was the only source of the fun, the relaxation on all those nights in - you are hooked to a belief that alcohol is your only source of relax, the birthdays, holidays, Christmas - the hook is that they wouldn't work without alcohol. Your story will have other unique hooks. Mine had associations with my past, with my children and my difficult life. What are yours?

Action point

Why have you given alcohol the starring role? Start to think about it. If you feel comfortable, start to write it down. Reflect on this power and this influence that you have given to alcohol. We will come back to this.

I could dwell on the damaging impact of alcohol's presence in society in a whole series of books. I have a lot to say on the subject, but this particular book isn't about the political debate around alcohol. I will be focusing entirely on the benefits of removing alcohol and my method of how to achieve that. This is a wholly positive guide to alcohol change, not because I am being unrealistic but because if you actually do live The Sober Experience for any length of time then that is the only way to describe it. I want you to feel empowered to remove alcohol if and when you choose, to enable you to see the parts of life that alcohol has been masking.

If you are stuck in an unwanted habit of drinking you already know it doesn't feel good, but focusing on that negative won't push you forward as it keeps your mind stuck back where you don't want to be. But change the focus to the present and how to get to the life where alcohol isn't in control, that is where the good stuff happens, and I will give you the tools and confidence to switch your mind into sober mode.

So, as I said I am going to take you on a journey, in a metaphorical sense as we plan, learn, pack, set off and explore the new destination. It is this process that helps to support that mind shift and create a life map where alcohol just isn't necessary or desired. It is the addictive aspect of alcohol that brings the need for a process not a quick fix.

Throughout my lifetime of exposure, I have gained an acute awareness of how alcohol can get into the front seat of your life, pushing you into the passenger seat. I see patterns of behaviour that hold people back and I see the lightbulb moments that eventually stick.

Removing alcohol gives you permission to do life differently. It is truly the best thing I have ever done for my life, and I have met and encountered thousands of people through sober groups who would say that very thing. That is why I want anyone that wants to experience alcohol free life too to feel empowered to make the change.

So, with the introductions out of the way, strap yourself in and let's begin.

My story

"One day you will tell your story of how you overcame what you went through, and it will be someone else's survival guide."
- Brené Brown

I'm sharing a high level version of my story because you may resonate with parts of it and with some of the roles I have played along the way, or simply with some of the emotions I have felt. I don't feel I have come to the point in my life where I can share the detailed version as it isn't just mine to share. My hope is that it might give you greater empathy and understanding for your own drinking patterns and struggles.

We can't be friends any more

Gradually I woke up to the fact that I was sitting in the backseat of my own life. Something else had taken the starring role. This was when I realised alcohol and I could no longer be friends.

The old me would have been terrified if you had asked me to navigate my life without alcohol. Alcohol had been a part of my life for three decades. I treated it like a trusted friend; always there, always available, no questions asked. I had never even attempted a single Dry January or Sober October and was proud of that fact. Because back then I saw doing one of these challenges as an admittance that I might have a problem. I couldn't see any other reason for doing it. I now view these challenges as an opportunity to get a taste of sober life! My drinking increased over the years, but I was still ticking enough of the essential boxes - family, children, work, friends, a nod to a hobby perhaps. No alarm bells were ringing. I was a NORMAL drinker. I felt no inclination to call myself otherwise.

On my 40th birthday I was just getting ready to ease myself into another decade of this NORMAL drinking when thoughts started popping into my head over a period of time. These thoughts became louder, and they all centred around one theme:

"Where did my life go?"

A strange feeling was beginning to surface. I don't know where it came from. Maybe it had been bubbling for years and my subconscious had suppressed it, but it genuinely felt like an entirely new feeling of something I can only describe as a mix of doubt, curiosity, realisation and a drop of fear. But before I move on here let me first rewind a few decades.

Exposure to alcoholism

As a child of two classically defined parents with alcoholism I had a very bleak and clear awareness of what a worst-case outcome looked like with alcohol. Alcohol destroyed the lives of my parents and wiped out the childhood of my brother and I. Huge chunks of my childhood are missing from my memory as a result of the trauma and many of the bits I do remember I often wish I couldn't. The upside to my childhood, I thought, was that from a young age I was aware of what I saw as the 'danger signs of alcohol. I felt sure that what happened to my parents would never happen to me. My own life would never be taken over by alcohol and if I had children, I would never put them through what I'd experienced. Convinced I was immune to the downside of alcohol, I promptly leapt into the 90s alco-pop era feet first!

Three decades of alcohol infused memories

I began drinking alcohol at 15. I initially used it to boost my confidence and to give me a sense of escaping from everyday life. I moved around a lot during my later teenage years and twenties - university, living in London with different jobs and in different house shares, and even a stint at travelling round the world. But wherever I went, alcohol always came with me. I never even questioned whether I really needed to drink on every single social occasion or whether I could try a night without it. I certainly never thought of trying an entire life without it! One of my frivolous aspirations for when I finally had a 'grown up' life was to have a kitchen with one of those second little fridges dedicated to my trusted friend, alcohol. To me, that was the height of kitchen cool!

Alcohol was completely ingrained in my mental processes. I don't believe my drinking consumption was unusually high. I was surrounded by regular drinkers like me. But I knew that I suffered more than some of my friends. I knew I drank more quickly than many and that drinking often triggered difficult emotions for me. I recognised that I had been through some tough times, but I never ever questioned whether for me, not drinking might be a better path to help me navigate life rather than the path I was taking, which I was aware was clearly using alcohol to escape. I knew I would often get pulled into a drunken haze of upset whenever I drank more than I could handle. I was also aware deep down that alcohol often took me to a place that could take a few days to recover from both mentally and physically (although I would insist to myself, I was fine the next morning – didn't we all!). I just never ever thought that these points might be a sign that I should consider a different approach. I was a NORMAL drinker and that overrode any signs of a problem.

If I had continued to narrow my gaze and focus solely on the alcohol buzz I got from possibly the first couple of drinks, I might never have seen a problem. Because it is what frequently happens outside of the brief period of warmth/buzz/hedonist vibe that we happily ignore or forget.

Mummy loves wine

I am not exactly sure when the concept of 'mummy with wine' slotted so comfortably into society. Wherever it came from I felt I was certainly a valid candidate - career mum, multiple children, child with additional needs, sensible abstinence whilst pregnant. I met the criteria, so off I went enjoying a decade of "well deserved" mummy wine. My thirties were possibly the most significant in ramping up my drinking volume as the opportunities were everywhere. It worries me just writing that - the decade with the most drinking opportunities/ justifications for me was my most significant parenting decade. How could that be? But it was and I wasn't alone in this. My social life 100% revolved around drinking due to the constraints of parenthood I suppose. Time was limited and outings difficult to arrange, so catching up over a drink became the norm. Strangely because children were involved, gatherings would often start early to accommodate the little ones but then not end any earlier. So, the drinking window widened on occasions. Combine that with a drink to unwind at the end of the day and slowly my drinking levels increased.

I look back now and think how much easier those parenting struggles would have been without alcohol. How much more rewarding the good times would have been without the alcohol fog. I wish I could shout that from the rooftops to every struggling parent out there! But for me, in the moment, it didn't feel like anything was wrong. If it did, I would have addressed it. It's only on reflection that I realise how much harder alcohol made life for me, and how only a part of me was showing up as a parent. It's only on reflection that I realise just because drinking is deemed perfectly "normal" it doesn't mean it doesn't impact us in some pretty significant ways.

I would like to introduce my middle daughter here. She was diagnosed with a rare chromosome disorder the April before she started school in 2014 and autism in 2024. Life up to that first diagnosis had been a battle of constantly questioning whether there was a delay with her development, and then trying to convince the medical professionals to act on our concerns. So, as anyone who has been down this road might appreciate, the years leading up to that diagnosis had not been without their struggles. But whilst finally getting a diagnosis was a relief, suddenly life felt a little blurred. The future disappeared in the sense of that "normal" (that word again) future where your children are transient both in your home and under your support and guidance. Because of the rareness of her disorder, the support and advice from Great Ormond Street Hospital was unfortunately limited as there were so few children that had been diagnosed with her specific condition. So, we were suddenly left with a total void. The future was unknown. Putting everything else aside, in terms of my alcohol consumption, I felt this definitely justified me to drink more. I now had my 'all access pass' to drinking to recover from struggles with my children. It wasn't a deliberate choice to behave like this. I genuinely think it's all around us - we are programmed to react by escaping. We are programmed to deserve reward. And isn't that exactly how alcohol is sold?

"ESCAPE AND REWARD"

Did I even have a choice? Of course I did. Not drinking would have been a choice. On reflection, for me, that would have been a much better path on so many levels, but I didn't become aware of it as an option until a few years later.

Valuing my self worth

After my daughter's diagnosis something in my mind solidified the 'mummy drinking' reward habit. There was just no question I would behave any differently. I wish I had valued myself more and recognised that the alcohol wasn't helping and what I really needed was self-care. I realise now, I hadn't really been taught self-care as a child, and I'd carried that forward into adulthood. This is a problem I know I am not alone in experiencing. It's a problem that I believe massively contributes to a reliance on alcohol which is why I mention it here in case it rings true for anyone reading this. I only learnt to be kind to myself in later life after counselling helped me come to terms with my past, and reflection helped me see the impact of that past. As long as my past had been sitting there in the frame surrounded by feelings of hurt, sadness, loss, anger, I had my permanent need to escape. But once I reframed it, I was able to start being kinder to myself. This is why I do mention therapy at times just in case this might be something you want to consider too.

To be honest, I think lack of self-care is a huge problem with parents generally, so my situation wasn't unique. Putting your children first is a natural priority and can leave you feeling like you have little time for anything else. When we are stretched trying to do it all and against the backdrop of seemingly incessant infant demands and emotions, the feeling of relaxation induced by a glass of wine can feel like a convenient and socially approved fix or remedy. But we don't pause to consider whether it can do more harm than good.

But I always found it was in the times that stirred up the strongest of emotions that managing my drinking consumption was the hardest. The more heightened my emotions, the greater volume I would consume to dampen them. On those nights, a "relaxed" evening would turn into a blur of sedentary inaction with all senses numbed. A "fun" night out would lead to potential memory loss or a stirring of negative emotion, and these nights would always be followed by a strained hungover morning.

But the weekly pick me up becomes a relied upon habit. The one glass multiplies, the one night increases to two or three as our baseline increases and we must drink more to get the same effect. Our brains normalise the level of drinking and seek more to keep getting the buzz. This is explained more in Lesson 1, where I explain more about the link between alcohol and the brain.

Thoughts emerging

The turn of a new decade, my 40s, triggered me to explore exactly that: how I felt outside of that moment - before, shortly after and then long-term after a few drinks. When I started to notice the impact alcohol was having on everything outside of that moment of consumption I was genuinely astonished. I would often not sleep well on drinking nights. I would feel slow the next morning. I might skip exercise, do less in my day than I would like, struggle to engage with people, struggle to focus at work, struggle with my emotions, struggle to do much at all. I would experience "hangxiety" - that horrible combination of feeling physically drained and extremely anxious from too much alcohol consumption (explained in Lesson 1). I had just never thought about all this before. Then of course there are the long-term health risks, the liver damage, brain damage, heart disease, links to cancer, impact on menopause for women, areas which I won't cover but which are well researched and documented. You might not need a liver transplant with the volumes you are drinking, but the physical impact is there for everyone. But unless the risks get to the extreme end of the spectrum (and even then it isn't guaranteed) this is rarely a driver to stop.

So, as I was writing this book, I concluded that alcohol consumption is a unique hobby. It is so incredibly popular, yet rarely does anyone question its negative effects. We talk about runners' knees, the dangers of skiing, the perils of road cycling, how a switch away from dairy might be more beneficial for our gut. We might ponder over veganism vs vegetarianism and various other health opportunities at great length, yet we leap into the drinking hobby blindly as countless people have done before us, and then we maintain the illusion by keeping the secret. We **insist** on our children wearing helmets to cycle, seatbelts in the car, and to cross the road when the pedestrian signal tells us, yet do we give them any warnings when they start drinking, and do we ever try to discourage them or highlight that alcohol isn't an essential part of life? On the whole we do not. We joke about coming of legal age and promptly hand them a pint of beer with a chuckle and possibly the words:

"your first of many I am sure."

We have all experienced nights when someone has had far more than they can handle, yet we never dwell on that. As I mentioned above, we rarely dwell on any negative consequences in fact. We somehow turn it around and laugh about how dreadful we feel, following it up with "great night though wasn't it" even though we might not be altogether sure it was. We happily encourage non-drinkers to drink, and we would expect alcohol to be provided at every social occasion or indeed any occasion where we are standing still for a few hours. It's like one big charade, and yet the moment someone goes over "the edge" we don't know how to handle it. They have a problem. They took it too far. Even though it's a highly addictive substance, it is their lack of control that is the issue. Even though there is no strict definition of what too far actually looks like! Even though there might be a compelling backstory to their increased consumption, it is still their lack of control that has got them to this point. It is deemed that suddenly they couldn't handle it. They are one of the few weaker ones.

But why is it so black and white as far as society is concerned? You can almost see the ledge and if you are unfortunate enough to fall off it you are banished until you can figure the problem out by yourself. You will unintentionally be left to feel ashamed, ignored, maybe quietly sympathised with. But you are unlikely to be supported as people don't feel fully comfortable yet talking about it. There are a huge amount of support services out there, but not everyone can find the strength to reach for those services or they feel because of the "normal" label those services aren't for them.

So, I guess that was the problem for me. There apparently wasn't one. No alarm bells were ringing.

"Society has created an environment where drinking is expected, not the anomaly"

Unless you disturb the happy vibe: that illusion of utopia that society has created around alcohol, then you are safe to crack on as I did. If you do start to stray into unpleasant territory, then you are asked to do it quietly so as not to upset the illusion.

Why do I labour the point here? I do it because I want to highlight why so many of us have fallen victim to the negative side of alcohol. The image lied to us, and we were already in too deep before we realised. You might have that feeling that you don't quite know how it got to that stage, "why me?," "why can't I handle my drink?", and I believe the reason is because it could happen to absolutely anyone.

Alcohol is a drug, and so as with any drug it will react differently for everyone as we are none of us the same. Our life make up is different, our perception of life, health, childhood, financial situation, place in society, environment, life events, physical traits. It all comes together to create us as individuals. So how can alcohol possibly affect us all in the same way?

I dwell on this point because I want you to know that I hear you. I dwell on this point because the story that society conveys is bonkers, and this means we have to double down our efforts to create that alternative story if the alcohol one isn't working for us. A more powerful story with a much better ending. I shall continue......

So, there I had it. I believed this vision of a happy alcohol consuming culture left only two sides of the fence: In control or alcohol dependent. No middle ground. You were either a normal drinker (that word again) or you had a problem.

"I believe that there is an element of fear around one side of the fence. We know that side destroys lives and is socially unacceptable so I would argue that we are almost forced to sit on the other side of the fence pretending we can handle our drink and that we are enjoying it."

Unbelievably when people stop drinking, other people's first thought is often, "are you an alcoholic?" The idea that you would actually simply choose not to drink just isn't considered!

Still sitting on the fence. Can I get off now?

I noticed this new category emerging around me - a middle ground between these two extremes I have mentioned - the "middle lane/grey area drinker". I am still not sure who fits into this group, but it seems to sit on the fence between "happy consumer" and "alcoholic." It is an attempt to acknowledge a group of people who drink above the recommended levels but wouldn't consider themselves risky. It's a pretty extensive group due to the fact that most people seem to dismiss the Government recommended drinking levels as unnecessarily low. For me, the greyness of this grey label has just confused things more and didn't really offer any solutions. But it was a contributing factor in making me realise I didn't want to be on the fence anymore. I no longer wanted to be the mummy that loved wine. And actually, while we are on the subject, did I really love it? The illusion was finally starting to slip. So, in a nutshell, after a 30-year stint at fully embracing alcohol into my life, I started to explore an alternative path and question who exactly defines the "normal" behaviour we all aspire to, and do I really actually care to conform anymore?

What signalled the change?

It's important to admit here that it wasn't one thing as such. I don't necessarily think many people do experience a lightbulb realisation, and I think waiting for one will really delay the departure date for this new Sober Experience. But as I said before, it did all revolve around me questioning the makeup of my life. It led me to begin to question how **I** actually felt

- me. I was suddenly interested in myself as an individual. Yes, I could drink wine in an evening and function fine at "life" the next day, but was it really enhancing it? Was it really "fine" if I was truly honest? Or had my definition of "fine" diminished into a tiny spec of my former existence to enable me to function with alcohol in my system? I couldn't put my finger on it, but it just started to feel uncomfortable. I started thinking that although we use the term "normal" to define our lives or aspects within it, I noticed that my own personal "normal" had reduced to a life that was pretty lacking. It happened slowly, so slowly in fact that I simply hadn't seen it. I realised I felt tired and uneasy on too many occasions and alcohol was the cause. I realised my mind was now perceiving alcohol as the only source of my **enjoyment**, my **unwinding,** my **escape.** I didn't just **feel** like a glass of wine anymore. More often I **needed** it and that started to worry me. I realised I didn't challenge myself in life anymore. My modus operandi was existing, not thriving. My family was my priority which was great, but because I wasn't firing on all cylinders, I wasn't showing up brilliantly for that role or anything else.

The symptoms of my drinking hobby

It took two years of pondering as I started looking a little deeper at this life of mine with all the boxes ticked, and realised I had a few worrying symptoms that together didn't paint the perfect picture of health and wellness. I have listed a few of them here as I know it is sometimes helpful to see a list:

- Lethargy

- Brain fog

- Using "a busy week" to justify relaxing with wine

- Desire to hurry kids' bedtime on occasions to get to my "mummy relax time"

- Mind space taken up by which nights I would drink

- Mind space taken up by how much I would drink so as not to be "excessive"

- Blinkered - I had my little world and hadn't ventured beyond it for some time

- Lack of energy the following morning

- Using alcohol as an evening coping mechanism for the day's stress

- Next day 'hangxiety'

- Drinking very much driven by emotions

- Emotions very much driven by drinking

You may well be able to relate to some of these symptoms and have a whole load more of your own perhaps. The more I thought about my life the more I realised it was insanity! I was regularly consuming something that was having such a negative impact on my life. Once the thought took hold, I couldn't get it out of my head, so why didn't I stop right away? Well, as I mentioned earlier when sharing about growing up in an alcoholic home, I had a very, very clear picture of when alarm bells should be ringing. I had still never displayed excessive drinking behaviour in front of my children as such. Neither had I ever had a drink in the morning (excluding airports – situational displays of early morning drinking in the UK seem acceptable). They were my go-to indicators that we might have a problem. I feel a bit crazy saying it now. Because I was so set on what the danger zone looked like, I never noticed I was drinking more than I wanted, despite not hitting those self-imposed warning levels. Combine this with lots of reasons why stopping drinking wouldn't work for me - believe me when you look for THOSE you will find them, and they will be loud! It actually hadn't dawned on me that there was another viable option! It hadn't occurred to me that too much for me might not look like someone else's capacity. My brain was attached to the habit and society's acceptance of the habit made me never question it. My drinking career had spanned thirty years. Stopping wasn't necessarily going to be an overnight success story.

So, if it wasn't an instant lightbulb moment what did happen? I remember my very first step clearly. As I mentioned, my thoughts changed as I entered that 40s decade, and I started to think maybe I didn't want to continue getting out of control drunk. This behaviour, if you call it, suddenly did not appeal to me at all. I picked nights when I knew I would have a tendency to drink excessively – big group nights, functions where I didn't feel 100% comfortable. If it was likely to be a "bender" I better avoid drinking at all. It felt strange at first, primarily because I didn't feel like I had an excuse for my abstinence – previous reasons being "I am on antibiotics" or "I am pregnant" or "I am running a marathon tomorrow." I think those were quite possibly the only reasons I had ever given in the past. "I just want to see what it's like to not drink" was a new one on me.

I was one of those drinkers who would NEVER, literally NEVER have just one. I drank for the buzz, I drank for this numbing feeling that I thought relaxed me, made me escape from the day. I had told myself my life was busy, tough, stressful (a word I am sure I overused to justify the drink) and that I deserved these nights out. The anticipation seemed to speed up my drinking, like I was already in motion when I left the house so I would hit the drinking at speed.

I realised I'd had nights out that I just couldn't remember – and plenty of them. I recalled nights out when I had to be walked home, nights out when I had taken a tumble, nights out when I had become uncharacteristically upset. There were plenty of uneventful nights too, but it was the nights that came with a bucketload of unwanted emotion that I was thinking about. I started to recall the following mornings: the horrific hangovers, hoping my children would have their first lie in, encouraging a movie morning so I could nurse my hangover slowly, telling the family we would have a chill day which basically meant I didn't have the energy for anything else. I also started to recognise that I had dreadful anxiety on many of those mornings.

So, that was the start for me. Try a few nights out without drinking.

The 28-day challenge

As the noise in my head grew louder, and as my discomfort around my alcohol consumption started to gather momentum, Facebook (as it has a frightening habit of doing) read my thoughts (literally) and one day an advert popped up for a 28-day challenge to give up alcohol. It came at the right time, and I was ready to try it. I joined a local community of alcohol-free adventurers. I immersed myself in quit lit (alcohol free literature), podcasts and learning. I felt myself starting to see, and then embrace a new existence that didn't revolve around alcohol. My mornings gradually became longer as I started to get up earlier. My evenings became freer and less noisy as thoughts were no longer dominated by all the alcohol questions: what time to drink? How much is too much? What days will I drink? Do I need to factor recovery time into my weekend? I did the challenge clinging like so many to the hope that 28 days would be the magic number. Well, it turns out 28 days is not a scientific number as such. It derives from the Minnesota model (1) that was developed in the US in the 1950s and was thought of as the adequate amount of time for a brain to recover and reset alongside additional support therapies. This number was then picked up by US health insurance companies who capped their insurance cover for alcohol services at 28 days and so this number stuck and spread around the world. It is not a magic number. Its research cohort was small. Other studies have found longer programs more beneficial. We are all different. We have all come to this point with a unique back story. One number will not fit all.

I did manage 28 days alcohol free challenge, and because at the time I believed it was indeed the 'magic number' I thought I had nailed it. Of course, for me and for many other people 28 days is achievable – that is not to discount the achievement by any means. But the way the mind works it see just four weeks and four weekends, and the end is clearly in sight when you start. I was excited to begin the challenge as it was something I'd thought about for a few years and it felt good to succeed. I relaxed, happy in the knowledge that I was capable of abstaining from alcohol and that I clearly didn't have a problem. That complacent attitude led to my returning to 'moderate' drinking (I discuss moderation in Part I) and then back to my regular drinking levels.

So, in an effort to initially avoid complete sobriety (and the reason for that I put down to fear which I later discuss), going alcohol free did not happen in a straight line for me. Something in that feeling of elation that I felt for not drinking for 28 days attached itself back to the buzz I got from drinking. Or maybe I thought I was fixed, that enough time had passed. It started with a combination of me pressing the f*ck it button when a bunch of childhood emotions surfaced around a family wedding, but also, I just wanted to find out if I really could have it all and moderate. Was I indeed fixed? On deciding I would try this moderation (explained in Part

I) I conveniently engaged my selective memory, removing all the negatives associated with my drinking.

I was back to my regular "normal" drinking habit pretty quickly. It turns out sticking to "reasonable limits," however you define them, is not easy when you are dealing with an addictive substance. I was gutted. This was not how I wanted my life to be now, and so I decided to go alcohol free properly again, but this time with learning. I went back through the process to remove alcohol entirely, for good this time.

A lesson learned

So, this was the absolute turning point. This was the point I realised what it was all about for me. I realised in my feeble moderation attempt that alcohol still did not deliver all that I told myself it had promised, that I would rather learn to face uncomfortable feelings and feel them entirely than drown them out and face the consequences. Life just improves when you remove the alcohol. The problems still come, but none of the extra alcohol fuelled ones. Sicknesses still happen, but not the alcohol induced sickness, and the recovery is so much quicker.

So, I would ask anyone that is curious about alcohol change not to try to label themselves, not to wait for a lightbulb moment, but just to ask themselves one question:

"Does alcohol really make me feel good?"

If the answer is "no" or even just "possibly not," now is the perfect time to grab that new energy and try life differently.

"But did you have a problem with alcohol?"

Ah, I never tire of that question! It isn't meant with malice. I have only ever received it with genuine curiosity, perhaps on occasion a desire on the part of the enquirer to benchmark their drinking habits against mine. No matter. At first the question floored me. Stammering a form of response, initially firmly denying any problem was the general knee jerk answer. "I just fancied a change." (Nothing to discuss here, please don't label me). But now I think it's important to own how I actually did define my own "problem" if you will.

"I believe it's a feeling not a label"

I don't like referring to it as a drink "problem." How can doing what is legally expected of me as an adult be defined as a problem? I also don't believe there was a label out there that matched my "symptoms". But I do think the lack of label here is the actual problem in a society that loves labels. As I mentioned earlier with the grey area drinker which comes with a pretty grey, non-committed description, without a clear label we are less inclined to seek a resolution. This is why losing the labels is #2 of my ground rules that follow.

But I did have a feeling. A feeling that I thought I had more to offer life, and life had more to offer me. A feeling that I could show up stronger for my children, my husband, my friends and my life. A feeling that I was pretty bored of that Monday morning repeated panic/sick feeling/exhaustion going into yet another week. A feeling that I perhaps guarded my bottle of wine sitting in the fridge a little too fiercely. A feeling that alcohol just wasn't delivering as promised.

Hello life!

This is how it genuinely felt for me. The very second you even question the impact alcohol might be having on your life, the blinkers start to lift. If you allow yourself to feel a gradual shift in the way you are thinking, to start asking questions, to not see everything as black and white, to start asking how you specifically are feeling, this will allow you to open the door to change and embrace the information that follows. And when you do start to ask questions, then your mind becomes flexible in other ways. When you do change your drinking habits positively you will find the positives just keep growing, especially when you continue to consciously look for them! My top three are reduced anxiety, hugely improved ability to cope with life and endless hours of extra time! You have yet to discover your top three!

Please remember you may not notice change immediately and this goes alongside why you might well re-read this book numerous times.

"You might not feel like that right away"

I would never want to diminish people's struggles and so right now you might feel anything but positive. But bear with me, I urge you. Keep reading. Alcohol heightens all the negative emotions. It adds fuel to the fire. Removing alcohol removes that huge added weight. But it takes time.

Whether you are with me yet or not, one thing that has supported me and I hope will support you is this:

"It was all learning, every bit of it."

The nights when (even though I had my warning level) I still did drink more than I would have liked in front of my children, the nights when I burst into tears and I just don't know why, the days that I lost to having no energy for my kids, the arguments with my husband because I felt so awful inside, the triggered memories of my own past. I feel so much stronger now to be able to say, "I deserve more than that." I feel so much stronger now that I can acknowledge how dreadful alcohol really did make me feel a lot of the time.

"I had reclaimed the lead role in my life"

This is how it genuinely felt. When you don't follow the dominant path and start to ask questions, then your brain becomes flexible in other ways. It starts allowing you to explore. Again, the open mindset emerging (explained in the next section). I don't want to waste time boring you with my sober story as I want us to get cracking on lighting your own fire. But in a nutshell, I got sh*t done, the pain moments have become more manageable as sobriety made me braver and my life has gained a lot more colour, and all it took was one change!

Just act on the feeling

So, if you also have a feeling or a seed has been planted then let's go! If alcohol has taken up too much space in your world, your life has the potential to be so much more colourful and so much bigger than it is now, and I say this with nearly five years personal sober experience at the time of writing this book and from having witnessed thousands of success stories in the groups I am a part of. If you compared my current life map with the drinking me, you wouldn't associate the two lives. I had never ever tried being alcohol-free before (aside from pregnancies). There was definitely a point when I thought sober people were boring. I am no Psychologist, but I bet in part I envied them as I didn't think I would be able to do it. I thought alcohol was a necessary part of me until I realised it wasn't and I did the work to make the change. Be kind to yourself and give it a try if it feels like alcohol isn't serving you.

The idea of changing or even challenging your relationship with alcohol can feel like a big ask. But if I invited you to pause, reflect and then explore your world outside of the initial alcohol buzz, you might just decide there is a whole lot of life that you are missing out on, and if you let that new life in, you may even start to notice the colour that was missing before.

Wherever you are right now, my intention is to guide you through a Sober Experience, and by the end of it how you decide to view alcohol will feel like a choice you can make.

Part I

Destination

There are three parts to this first section.

1. Let's first acknowledge **why do we drink?** and the impact it has on us. Honest awareness and conversation around alcohol is the key to change.

2. Then we explore what the **gains** are from not drinking.

3. We finish with setting the **Ground rules** for the experience.

Why do we drink?

If we don't want to drink so much, why do we? It must be a habit right? What motivates the habit?

A desire to experience pleasure or escape discomfort that we have told ourselves alcohol will fix.

This is the pleasure pain principle (1) and the driving force behind human behaviour. The theory is that nothing we do is random. There has to be a reason for it, and if we can identify your reasons for drinking this will help.

> **Action steps and journal prompts**
> **What is the discomfort you are trying to alleviate or the pleasure you are seeking?**
> An answer may not spring to mind instantly. Take the time to think about it. Is it boredom, loneliness, relaxation, do you want to numb an experience or maybe it's something else? The habit has formed because your mind has told you that alcohol is fulfilling a need, and if done regularly enough, your brain adapts to the constant presence of alcohol and then itself needs the habit just to feel "normal" because your baseline has increased.

We need to identify the cause if we are to move away from it. You might not know why you are drinking as much as you are. Yes we know it's addictive but there is usually a point that triggers a shift in volume, a shift in regularity. Again, I'd suggest you reflect on your own triggers - maybe a stressful job, a relationship breakup or family pressures. If you write it down something might well come up.

Life never stays the same. What was once an occasional drink to relax after your week at work might turn into a more regular drink to recover from the struggles of a life shift. We move into a new phase so often. Acknowledging that a life shift has led you to increase the amount you drink might just be the realisation that you need. You might well have been managing your drinking at the outset or for many years, but it's okay to acknowledge something has changed.

How to become sober when you are in a dark place

Life can be bloody tough. Life can challenge us. I write this paragraph for those that are struggling with painful lives right now. Then add in trying to remove alcohol and/or other drugs, and you might feel helpless, like you are fighting an uphill battle. It can be so difficult to let go of what you perceive to be your only glimmer of enjoyment, relief, release, numbing. The element of fear might creep in - fear that you might not be strong enough. It can be so difficult to avoid temptation when you are surrounded by others continuing the habit and it isn't that easy to just avoid them. I hear you, I really do, but I tell you this thing, this crutch, this reliable friend - it doesn't help. It's an illusion. So, when I ask you to change your thoughts but you struggle to identify with my line of thinking, because frankly you have other things to worry about, just humour me. Whatever your current struggle, whether it's a stressful job, family pressures or a world rocking event, removing alcohol will improve your ability to cope with it. You will feel more able to take tiny steps forward, experience those vital first glimmers of positivity.

Your shrinking world

Regularly drinking excessively is bad for your health. We all know this. But as I acknowledged in my story, are we really honest about what point the damage starts to show? I now believe the recovery period from any pattern of drinking, whether it's a binge now and again or a regular but more moderate amount, can have such a negative physical and mental impact that it can leave you with no choice but to take a supporting role in your own life, as the effect is so significant it eats into huge chunks of your available time and can play havoc with your mind and body. Your mind is capable of running on autopilot, in fact it seeks autopilot if it is struggling. So you may have been keeping up with the essential life commitments: work, children, life admin etc., thus being fooled into thinking you weren't being impacted by your alcohol consumption. But there is a very big BUT! The underlying impact that alcohol might be having on you means you won't have capacity for much more so anything else goes out the window, and worse, what you are achieving is just grey. You are showing up but in miniature form. You are delivering but with a tiny voice. You are present yet not really. So it is a trade-off and if you think it is worth it on certain occasions then that's great, but if you are realising it isn't worth it or actually those occasions are more habitual than you had at first noticed, or those occasions trigger you to spiral, then let's act on that.

This might feel like an exaggeration to you or you might instantly relate. You might not have seen it like this but are starting to now. So why not stop and think about your own life right now:

"What if life could have more colour, more energy, more purpose?

What if removing one thing from your life could be the rocket fuel you need to do life differently?"

When we think about alcohol and whether we are drinking too much it is rarely an instant question and answer, because it isn't normally black and white. Society has normalised alcohol consumption to the degree that we are expected to drink it. This poses a problem because it masks the ability for people to seek help. As we already discussed, the word on the street is loud and clear - you are either an alcoholic or you are not, and as long as you are not you are just fine. So, society makes us feel uncomfortable about seeking help - you don't have a right to question your drinking habits unless they are "really serious." So, we need to step back a minute and ask ourselves,

How do "I" feel? / Is alcohol serving me?

Some possible signals

- If you depend on a glass of wine to rescue you from a negative mood

- If you drink to forget

- If you drink to cope with a life change, shock, trauma

- If you drink to overcome depressive feelings

- If your overall mood after drinking is one of regret, shame, anxiety, physical exhaustion

- If you can't have "just one"

- If you can't manage social situations without it

- If you seek more energy

- If you would love a life shake-up

- If you feel as though your life has diminished, leaving you just enough energy to function and keep drinking

If any one of these points resonate with you, or if you connect with any of the points in my story, or if something else has flicked a switch then let's get cracking.

What will I gain if I quit?

Well the list is endless and we have already mentioned some of the benefits. The gains will of course also be personal to you but here are a few that I have noticed for starters:

- Reduced anxiety

- Improved sleep

- No brain fog

- No lost hours

- Increased confidence - believe me

- Improved health

- Improved relationships

- Improved outlook on life

- Reduced depressive feelings

- Improved work concentration

- Improved work performance

- No wasted "recovery" time

- More observant

- Able to cope with life's ups and downs better

- More even tempered

- More money - alcohol is expensive!

- More grateful - this is a personal one, but I am so much more grateful as I am so much more present in my life

What you might lose?

To keep it balanced of course I must acknowledge here any potential downsides to removing alcohol, although I have to chuckle when I write that as I don't personally believe there are any. But if you are new to this the following have been highlighted as possible concerns when one might be considering navigating a path without booze, and I have to address them as I don't want them to pose as a barrier further down the line, but when I address them I will provide the counter argument:

Instant relaxation - alcohol increases the inhibitory neurotransmitters in the brain which help you feel relaxed - and if you continued to only receive more of that feeling I wouldn't have written this book. You can still get to that relaxed feeling but might have to work at it in the early days. Alcohol is a chemical stimulant that can temporarily override any natural reward pathways, but this is reversible. You can learn other natural ways of relaxing, such as exercise, yoga or meditation, or just being less busy. Alcohol removes the noise so I would argue it reduces the feeling you need to "relax" as you will naturally be less agitated without it. Plus the addictive element in alcohol makes you feel you "need" to relax.

Confidence - the increase in GABA, the relaxing neurotransmitter in the brain (discussed in Lesson 1), can create a feeling of confidence. But it's a false confidence that comes from numbing your senses and emotions. And over time many people find they have to increase their alcohol consumption to get the same effect. In a later lesson I explain that the confidence you gain from that sober clarity far outweighs the perceived alcohol confidence.

Escape - the feeling of escape is so short lived and comes at a massive price as consumption increases and emotions become more volatile.

Potential impact on social life - it is true that most people only associate the social experience with drinking so you might worry you will become a social recluse. I have found the opposite to be true and am busier than ever, finding new and interesting ways to socialise. You become so much more creative when you stop drinking because you feel free.

We discuss all of these pros and cons again in Lesson 5 and 6.

What does the Sober Experience involve?

- Bring an open mind and lose any "all or nothing thinking." Just go with the flow of the book.

- Be open to the suggestions I make and try to absorb the information I give you.

- Be honest with yourself.

- If you lose the thread just pause and repeat a section with which you do resonate.

- If you take a couple of days away from the book, consider going back a chapter and refresh if you need to.

- Buy a notebook. The process of writing can be so helpful when it comes to processing your thoughts and feelings. There are journal prompts throughout the book which essentially mean writing down your thoughts around the questions to trigger positive outcomes.

Positivity is the common theme because wherever you are in your life right now, having read this far means a seed of willingness to explore the Sober Experience has been planted. That is a powerful step.

This is more than giving up drinking

It has to be, or it won't work, but I want you to view that as a real bonus to the Sober Experience. We are creating a new life map, a new way of living. Removing the alcohol is just the catalyst. I could write you out the steps on one page but it's the context behind the steps that is important to digest. This is where I will introduce you to four theories to support the change. Your mindset will start to shift and open up and you will see two things working together: the alcohol removal and a complete life shift.

But you will need to get stuck in with me and then positive change will happen. So there are a few rules before we get started....

Ground rules to make this work

Let's work together on this one and let's be honest. At this moment it is likely alcohol is an unwanted habit for you, but because of its addictive component you will need to be proactive about this Sober Experience. You might find it harder than you thought, or you might breeze into sobriety because

"everyone's sunshine looks different"

We all have a different story, a different makeup. Stepping into the Sober Experience might lead you down a number of different paths. Some will stick and some will challenge you. But please be brave and throw everything into it. Whatever your reasons for being here, I would absolutely love you to make the most of it so let's set some ground rules:

- **Lose the labels:** society loves to label. It makes us feel safe. It reassures us and gives us a set of rules to conform to. We feel comfortable that way. But when it comes to alcohol I believe the labels prevent the conversation from flowing, as we are all focusing on putting ourselves in little boxes and we struggle when we can't find an appropriate box. So don't worry about what level of drinker you are. It doesn't matter. If the amount you are drinking doesn't feel right for you that is enough. There is no judgement or expectation here. This is your space.

- **Really understand that your urge to drink is only partly physical and the rest is mental and emotional**. The physical compulsion to drink passes relatively quickly. We are left with the mind and its association to alcohol. but you still have to deal with the more challenging mental and emotional aspects. This is covered in in Lesson 2.

- **Remember drinking is but a momentary fix drowning in potential problems:** when life is tough alcohol provides you with that f*ck it button. It's an internal cry for help. A declaration that life is just not fair, and it often feels that way whether you drink or not. But until you are honest about what alcohol can really do about it nothing changes. If you label it as your escape button then that is where it remains in your mind.

- **Rose tinted glasses:** When you are triggered your mind can choose to remember only the good times with alcohol - and the memories of the difficult times and hangovers shrinks. But be honest. If you find yourself putting on rose-tinted glasses, pause for a moment and remember the whole picture of how you felt when you drank. There's no need to dwell on the memory - just don't airbrush it.

- **Don't make it all about the alcohol:** if you focus on the alcohol aspect alone there can be a tendency to follow the mind path that convinces you that you are missing out. But removing the alcohol gives you the most amazing opportunity to boost every other aspect of your life and, actually, I believe that is the key to succeeding. If you keep thinking about the alcohol and introduce nothing else, all that you are faced with is on the one hand - the alcohol you are trying not to drink and on the other - a massive void. We need to remove that void, to fill any emptiness that, in the short-term, we might feel that alcohol has created. We need to change the map. Someone once quoted to me:-

"insanity is doing the same thing over and over again and expecting different results" (attributed to Einstein).

You need to make your life different in as many ways as you can. Our brains create paths. There is currently a powerful path in your head that leads straight to drink. That needs to be re-routed. Make life interesting. You are going to have to try new things and you should quickly learn that you enjoy the change.

- **It's not about what you don't want to do:** you need to feel positively ready. If an attempt to quit feels like it might be a knee jerk reaction to a recent unpleasant episode, you are going in with a negative head and it won't work. For example if another awful hangover and memories filled with a night of heavy drinking are your reasons to stop, hangovers fade so the reason loses its weight rapidly.

So instead, what do you want to get out of this? What might life look like? What are all the benefits that not drinking can give you?

- **You have to want the outcome more than you want the drink**: this is with anything you want to stop - sugar, alcohol, TV, food, overspending. You name it. We talked about outcomes further on, but if you don't make them more compelling than a drink this won't work. Keep your eyes on that. What are you already noticing if you have a stint under your belt? Always reflect on the positives, the reasons why stopping drinking would be so much better for you than continuing drinking.

- **Don't worry about getting to a certain point:** be it a certain number of days or months. This can be daunting and on tougher days, feel unachievable and therefore be a reason to abandon the plan. Focus on one day at a time. How do you want to feel today? Reflect on how good it felt yesterday to not drink. Or if you did drink yesterday, how is today/tomorrow going to be different?

- **Don't compare yourself: we are triggered to drink for so many reasons:** environmental, genetic, social, economic. Everyone's combination of factors is totally different. Never compare yourself. You are you, creating your own unique map, taking learning from sources that will support you, bolstering those trigger moments and using whatever tools you need to get the result you want.

Write down your learning and write down your whys

There are exercises throughout the book and it will support the experience if you can take part in them, and note down the changes along the way.

Action steps and journal prompts

Write down your whys: This is a big step for some people as it provides a focus point, so if you are able, write down a list of positive why's – reasons **why** you want to stop drinking?. Focus on those as we set off. That might feel difficult right now as you might have a recent negative experience sitting in your mind, but come back to this point when you feel ready. Be focused on an outcome: those why's need to be positive and about what do you want to gain? energy, focus, mental strength, physical fitness, more energy for your family - spend some time picturing the YOU without alcohol and what they look like. This visual can be so powerful and you can use it whenever you feel the pull to drink.

This is a positive Sober Experience: imagine doing one thing that could have the most incredibly positive impact on your life. Keep repeating this. It might not always feel like it, but keep telling yourself "this is a positive experience", whether it's having the energy to go on a walk every day, to start reading, to meet new people, to put yourself to bed properly at night, to brush your teeth every day, to recognise a sunrise, these are uncharted waters and they are positive. You might even climb a mountain or you might just realise you can climb the stairs more easily! It's your experience.

If you find yourself struggling on a particular day then come back to these rules. They should ground you.

Uncomfortable feelings bubbling up

Feeling overwhelmed - where to start? What do I need to do? Am I overreacting? I don't know if I can do this. So many questions.

Fear of what lies ahead and lack of clarity - this is a huge barrier. You just don't know what a sober future looks like and that is daunting and this is what I am talking about here. Let's start thinking about what we are aiming for and what it might look like. We cover this a lot more later on.

Being swept back into the social pull - "everyone knows we would all rather be drinking" can be a thought that is hard to let go of. You feel you are doing this because you have to, not by choice. Again, it is fear blocking you from thinking in a different way. Just be open minded and allow that thought pattern to change. It's okay to start out like this because socially you might not know any different. But as we start looking at all of the gains this thought pattern will change.

I can't imagine I will never drink again: So, don't imagine that. Focus on right now. Don't think long term. You might just be reading this book out of curiosity for now so you can park those questions for the moment. But if you are keen to succeed with this Sober Experience, then answering these questions will start you thinking and getting your mind on board. Please come back to them every now and then when you find yourself questioning yourself.

Any determination you feel might be strong and then fade at times of the day or week, or as time goes on. If your determination starts to fade, make a conscious effort to bring it back. Don't let it slip away. Don't do nothing.

Some terminology

Habit vs addiction

Two terms you often hear around alcohol. Let's understand them:

Habit: "a repeated action or a way of acting that is done regularly, sometimes without conscious awareness"

Addiction: "the inability to stop using or doing something, especially something harmful."

So one is done regularly, possibly without awareness and with the other there is lack of control and acknowledgement of harm. It's the fact that a habit can become unconscious, I believe, which explains how a person can slip into more of an addictive pattern without realising, without being aware, and it's because it's addictive that of course then makes it difficult to stop.

I think somewhere in the middle of those two definitions would sit the category of "unhealthy habits", but just looking at these two definitions together is really powerful. When I reflected on my alcohol story, I realised most of the drinking years were genuinely out of habit. It was drinking to fit in. It was drinking to feel "normal". It was basically drinking because no one gave me a reason not to. I could have probably stopped at many points along the way if I really needed or wanted to. So that, combined with the fact I hadn't allowed myself to think it was harming me, makes it a habit - the fact that I could control it but was doing it regularly. But somewhere along the line I would say it moved towards the definition of addiction - when I actually needed alcohol to fix me, to be "social me", to be "relaxed me". By then the habit had indeed become so "habitual" that my brain had normalised my drinking levels and so my baseline increased: I explain this later in Lesson 1 but I needed more to get the same effect as my brain had become used to it. But I was starting to acknowledge that it wasn't doing me any good and carried on anyway, and that is when I believe you can use the word addiction.

When something becomes a habit it becomes uncomfortable when we don't do it. When something moves from a habit to an addiction it literally becomes impossible not to do it, even though we know it isn't good for us. It's okay to use the term "addiction". It just helps to acknowledge how easily alcohol can become an unwanted, uncontrollable part of our lives. If we used the term addiction more openly we would highlight the dangers of alcohol more firmly.

I know for some of us this drinking thing might still be a habit or it might have crept into addiction territory. I am going to refer to it as a habit for the rest of the book. The word addiction doesn't work for many people as we have made it a taboo word in society, so I will stick to habit, but it refers to both here and I personally feel comfortable with both terms.

The spectrum of Alcohol Use Disorder

A new term has been created to combine the previous terms "alcohol abuse" and "alcohol dependence".(2)

> Alcohol Use Disorder (AUD) is a pattern of drinking that causes health problems or distress (NHS). AUD can be categorised as mild, moderate or severe . The UK Government expands on that to include any alcohol use that results in significant health risks or harm.

This medical term suggests that everyone who drinks over the recommended levels is on a spectrum. The key element is that of control - the inability to stop or control your level of drinking would put you on this spectrum. My question is, when do you become aware or allow yourself to acknowledge when that element of control is lost?   As I mentioned in my own story, I didn't acknowledge that alcohol was harming me, and I wasn't actually in control of my drinking until much later on.   But it's useful to be aware of the terminology and the attempts at widening the scope of individuals who should consider seeking support.   If the labels exist they need to be understood and they need to be there to support people.

Moderation

> Moderation: the quality of doing something within reasonable limits

I mention moderation here.   I understood moderation in the sense of it being able to drink a "reasonable" amount, but no one has properly defined reasonable, apart from the Government Alcohol Consumption Guidelines (see Appendix I) which are so often ignored, and actually if you drink regularly, this idea of moderation is really hard to achieve due to alcohol being so addictive.

When you are 'moderating' your drinking, boundaries are unclear and it's easy to slip up. Alcohol is always lurking in the background like a forbidden shadow.

Absolutely there are plenty of people who are able to drink in controlled amounts. But I wouldn't say they are moderating. They are just able to drink when they feel like it, but they don't drink often, and they don't drink habitually. They don't drink to fix a problem, and they can literally take it or leave it. If you told this group of people tomorrow that they would never be able to drink again they would be probably fine with that.

But moderation is something else. I believe moderation with alcohol is a conscious effort to drink less than you really want, and that can become a constant battle. If you previously used alcohol to change a mood or to change your state and it became your only way to do that, then moderation is always on your mind - "when can I safely drink again? Can I use one of my drinking nights tonight instead? Would that be a waste?" You might unconsciously categorise your non-drinking nights as less enjoyable, almost writing them off in your mind because you focus on the drinking nights. You are moderating but in doing so you diminish the enjoyment of the non-drinking evenings. If this is where you end up, then you aren't getting the full benefit from not drinking - not even close. Because there is no freedom. I talk about this in Lesson 9. The full benefit is seeing all that you can get out of life, not diarising your fulfilment for three nights a week and pining for those "special" nights the rest of the time.

The question of moderation crops up ALL THE TIME in sober circles. So many aspire to this lifestyle (?), of having "the best of both worlds," others lament that this just isn't on the cards for them. I ask you to consider looking at it from my perspective. I am so glad now that moderation is not for me. I am relieved that I don't have to debate with myself each week about which nights I will drink, how much I will consume etc. I am glad that I don't have to rate nights out to see whether they are worthy "drinking nights." I can just enjoy the night for what it is - connection with people I want to see. I am happy that I no longer have ANY of the ill-effects of alcohol. However small they appear to be at moderate levels they are still there. I now choose not to moderate. I choose to embrace life, to face challenges and to enjoy moments with 100% clarity of mind and being all into the Sober Experience feels so much more energising than calling myself "the moderator". As long as moderation is there, there will be the pull to alcohol whenever your emotions are challenged.

Part II
Knowledge

So, we have considered how easily alcohol can take up space in our world and how we live in a world that actively encourages drinking. I have suggested that, like for me, that path to excessive drinking might have arrived gradually and unnoticed, that the blurred line between habit and addiction played its part. I have asked you to consider how determined you are to succeed with this and to visualise what that looks like, with the acknowledgement that you might not yet know, and that's okay. And finally, we looked at our ground rules, as these need to be front of mind before we move on.

Now we start shifting our thought patterns and taking action. We are gathering and packing (the knowledge) for our experience. Now I introduce you to four concepts that will help you to start thinking in a different way. Because the resistance to change all comes from the thoughts. The physical cravings pass quickly for most people. We need to get your mind on board and these theories really help to completely shift the mindset so we can tackle your craving for alcohol. The logic will become clear as you progress.

The Monkey mind

It's the monkey on your shoulder that puts a drink in your hand before you even noticed you were craving one. It is essential that we get to know him!

The theory is that we all have within us the mind of a monkey. First mentioned by the Buddhists, the monkey mind describes the constant stream of irrational thoughts that run through our minds.

The Chimp Paradox by Professor Steven Peters (1) takes a different spin on this Buddhist concept. Peters describes the presence of our different brains - the chimp, the computer and the human and how they influence our mind.

- **The human** - is our conscious thinking system in the brain. It is you, your values, the way you want to live your life. It is logical, rational and factual. It wants to do the right thing, and it likes to plan.
- **The chimp** - is irrational in thought. It is quick to react and driven by emotion. You can't control when it pops up, but you can learn to reason with it and change its mind. The chimp will tell you you need a drink when you don't want one. We talk a lot about the impact of the chimp when we move onto the mind section, but for now I just want you to have an awareness of him in context with the other two brains.
- **The computer system** - this is the library for the human and the chimp. It is where you store routines and beliefs when they have been vetted and agreed by the human. The computer also stores memories. Currently your computer has several misconceptions surrounding the subject of alcohol. The computer will have automatic defaults that lead it to drinking. The computer will have distorted memories that are biased to the positive. I hope your computer will be deleting a lot of those unhelpful files as you are reading.

I want you to bring this monkey mind concept on board as we progress through this experience. I will ask you to engage your human at times. Don't forget your human brought you to this book. Your human wants you to experience a period without alcohol. If we can acknowledge who is talking at certain times, we can switch from chimp mode into human mode more easily.

***

Internal Family Systems

Imagine if you could see wobbles or triggers as being felt by a tiny part of you, not your entire self? Would that feel less overwhelming?

Internal family systems is a theory which was created by Richard C Schwartz in the 1980s (2). It is actually a form of therapy, but I have found it so useful in the context of changing your relationship with alcohol.

This is a type of therapy that believes we are all made up of several parts or sub-personalities

The idea is that we are not mono minded, but that we are made up of different parts that support us in functioning day to day. We are not just one being. Behind the parts is the "self" which is our ideal being so to speak. But that self is supported by our parts. The parts are made up of three types:

The managers: they keep us on track - they manage our behaviour and keep us behaving in a controlled manner. They make judgements based on our beliefs, culture etc. You could say the manager parts are run by your human brain and kept in check by your computer. Your managers will be on board with you stopping drinking as they want to protect you.

The firefighters: they step in when they are worried that we might be in danger or vulnerable in any way. They are spontaneous and impulsive - think your chimp! It is the firefighters that would lead us to drink to protect us from pain.

The exiles: I won't focus on these parts here, but they are the parts that would have been buried due to trauma and can be supported through specific therapies.

There are so many parts that come out when you are trying to make a change, any change, but in this case alcohol change:

- the parts of you that instigate the change - the healthy parts, the growth parts.

- the parts that relate to the change: those that can relate to the life after the change, to a vision of the new life.

- the parts that connect with your human and know that staying in the current state isn't going to give you the best future.

But there are the parts of you that still want to stay in the comfort of the old life, the drinking life and they aren't comfortable with this process yet:

- the parts that might connect the change with some sort of loss.

- the parts that associate alcohol with fun, confidence.

So instead of any "all or nothing thinking", of seeing slip-ups or blips as "failures", of seeing anything but an enormously long stint without alcohol as defeat, you can recognise the parts of you that embrace the change and the parts that we need to work on.

On board parts

Let's look at those parts of us that are on board with this experience, the parts that are already rooting for you to succeed. We are all different, but I will throw out some ideas:

the parent - Think about the parent part of you if you are one, the mum or dad who knows that they are showing up to the role with more clarity, with more energy, with their priorities better aligned. Notice as you continue with this experience how differently you are able to show up in that role.

the advice giving and listening friend - As the fog lifts you may find you lend more patient ears to your friends. Do you make more time for people, or do you think you could? Do you give better, more considered advice?

the more productive employee - Do you feel you show up to work differently now? With more clarity, more positivity?

the adventurer - Have you explored beyond your normal boundaries? Have the blinkers been lifted? Are you open to exploring?

Stuck parts

You may have some firefighter parts that are stuck in the past as a reason for making you drink. You may have initially started drinking when you needed confidence - as an awkward teenager and the label has just stuck. You never questioned it. Or when you started your career, you felt it was socially expected amongst work colleagues. Drinking may have been triggered by your firefighter as an essential element to support you in a situation and the habit remained. So, there could be many reasons you started drinking, but that doesn't mean you need to drink now.

Stuck parts will also be those that still associate drinking with certain elements of their personality or behaviour - the confidence giver, the relaxer etc. We challenge these parts in Lesson 6.

In order to free those stuck parts, we need to reassure them that the reason they used for drinking before no longer applies to their current life.

Action steps and journal prompts

1. Identify the stuck parts and talk to them
2. Why do you need that drink?
3. Do you really think you will stop at just one?
4. What else is the part telling you?

Room for all parts

Let's make room for all the parts, not just the ones that were already on this journey. With all the best intentions, life will throw unexpected curve balls, and we have to deal with them. Look at your parts as signalling you to make a shift. Let's bring back the chimp here and see the two as coming out at different times. Your chimp might be the gentle whisper in your ear to say "listen, if you sit on the same sofa after the same day at work you know I am going to suggest you have a drink".

The Firefighter might come out if it feels the situation demands it. On a night our if your mind gets locked into the idea that alcohol = fun and sober =boring, or 'I need a drink to calm my nerves' then acknowledge that that impulsive part of you is trying to take control, but there's no need to act on it. You are okay, it's just a bit of emotional discomfort and you can work through it.

So, these are all just signals, signals warning us that things aren't as they were, that situations aren't playing out like they used to and so your mind tries to tell you they need to be fixed.

Your human or your manager parts just need to send the message back that YOU ARE OKAY. This might take time.

***

The Cycle of Change

Making any change takes time. It is a process and acknowledging where you are in that process can support you in knowing what to do next.

You might be reading this book and feeling uncomfortable, worried, not ready yet. You might not progress as quickly as you would like, or you might embrace all the learning right from the start. Everyone comes to the process from a different perspective, with a different history and most importantly, being at different points in their life so it is helpful to look at the cycle of change, (3) a popular change model.

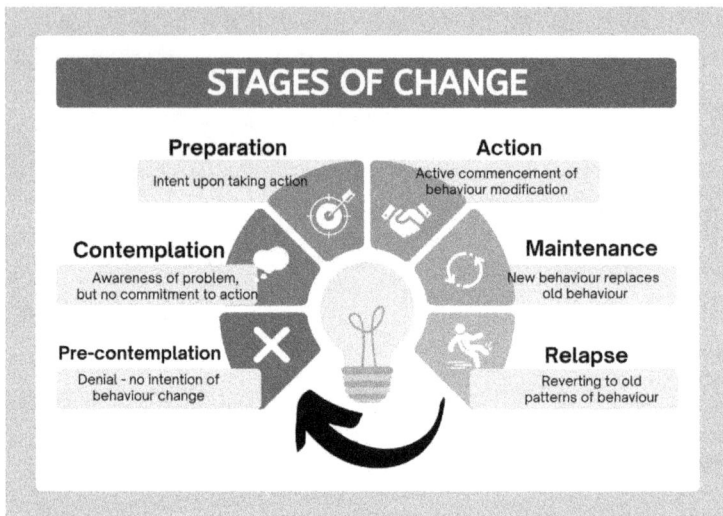

STAGES OF CHANGE

Preparation
Intent upon taking action

Action
Active commencement of behaviour modification

Contemplation
Awareness of problem, but no commitment to action

Maintenance
New behaviour replaces old behaviour

Pre-contemplation
Denial - no intention of behaviour change

Relapse
Reverting to old patterns of behaviour

If you understand where you are on the cycle, you might relate more to the way you are feeling right now. So, take some time now to see where you might sit. There are many drawings of this model that add on bits along the way, so I have picked this one.

Where do you sit on the cycle of change?

Pre-contemplation: this is that state you sit in before you even consider not drinking. You aren't even aware of this as an option for you. You are carrying on in your normal life.

Contemplation: the seed is being planted. You are opening your eyes to the problem or to the potential benefits change would bring. Thoughts are popping into your head, and you are pondering them.

Preparation: here you find books to read, groups to join, podcasts to listen to. You buy alcohol free drinks if they appeal to you. You make sure you are okay with your upcoming calendar, or you shift a few things around. You are getting ready.

Action: this is you starting to implement the steps, engaging in the exercises and other books and podcasts.

Maintenance: this crucial stage looks at you taking continued action with this experience. Not to constantly check in with the alcohol past at all. I don't believe this is necessary. But to keep boosting the new you, by continuing to change the map in a positive direction.

Relapse: this is addressed in Lesson 7. I don't call it relapse in the lesson as I frame it as learning. It is when you have been temporarily pulled back to drinking.

It is common to yoyo between contemplation and pre-contemplation as your human and chimp battle it out to dominate your actions. Your human contemplates the damage alcohol is doing, and your chimp pulls you back to pre-contemplation as, in that moment, the habit becomes too strong to break.

So, no matter how desperately you might want something, how important it is to you on the face of it, **change** can be really difficult if you don't tackle it the right way. I want you to understand this at the outset, so you ensure that you work at this and are successful. There are a few reasons people keep going round the cycle of change:

1. **Lack of understanding** - not fully understanding where the pull to drink comes from and why it is so difficult to stop. I will help with that in the book in Lesson 1.

2. **Fear of the unknown** - we discuss this throughout, but fear can be a huge obstacle for your mind. Listening to the many sober podcasts and reading books of people's individual experiences can help with this. I want to help alleviate those fears. We can do this together.

3. **Forgetfulness** - re-painting the picture over time so the original pain point is reduced or even completely eliminated, and you are once again left with that false rosy image of drinking.

4. **You don't want to change because:**

- **You are making alcohol a bigger part of who you are** - your ego thinks that alcohol represents you, is a necessary part of your life etc......

- **You are inflating the benefits** - this leads to ambivalence which we discuss in Lesson 6.

- **You don't know how to incorporate the change** - the social impact etc. - again fear of the unknown.

Understanding where you are on the cycle and why can support you in taking the next step. The process of stopping drinking can really pull you into the loop because it is addictive, pure and simple. Questioning the thoughts, being honest about what is pulling you to drink helps to remove the mask and expose alcohol for what it is - an unwelcome guest!

***

The Growth Mindset defined

Can you imagine trying to make a change if you aren't able to open your mind to new possibilities? This is why it is important to adopt a growth mindset here.

I talk about this concept as it is pretty crucial to changing your relationship with alcohol. Remember all those visions we have around alcohol. The associations with fun, the social insistence that we drink, the worry that we won't manage without alcohol in our lives. These are all imposed on us, and we have accepted them because we have adopted the closed mindset when it comes to alcohol. We have chosen to close our mind off to any other thoughts, any other logic, because it suits the habit. So how do we change our mindset when it comes to drinking? How do we move beyond all those thoughts that tell us we should be drinking? We need to adopt the growth mindset (Carol Dwek) (4).

The growth mindset suggests that

- If you put effort in you can initiate change

- That outcomes are not fixed

- This is all learning - with regards to alcohol if you stumble what can you learn? How can you do it differently?

Whereas with a fixed mindset

- You give up easily

- You avoid the challenge

- You put in no effort

What I want you to see from this is that the process to alcohol change is just that - a process and within that we will learn along the way, so you need to be open to that. So, if we engage in the Sober Experience by embracing the challenge element, being strong when facing setbacks, and putting effort in to get where we want to be, we are far more likely to succeed. Seeing the description of the two mindsets right there shows how we clearly need the growth mind to succeed in the Sober Experience.

So, first off just be curious! Curious and open to what I have to say.

***

Why are these theories important?

When you are in an unwanted habit of drinking there must be two forces pushing against each other or you would have stopped by now if that was your choice. There is the force that encouraged you to pick up this book - the force that wants to make a change, and there is the opposing force that is making it so difficult to successfully implement that change. So, we have to think how then do we succeed? By learning how these theories might support you we are shifting the power. There are book references on these theories on my website if you are interested to explore further as I only explore them in brief.

The Caveats

The need for therapy might come up

Therapy can be a huge boost to this Sober Experience for some people. So often a drinking habit forms on the back of trauma. If you feel this might be the case for you, then it might be a good idea to investigate some form of therapy. It really worked for me, and I have seen it work for so many individuals. I embarked upon counselling before I realised I wanted to stop drinking. It helped me make sense of a previously blurred past. I mention it here because you might find you struggle if this element is missing, so bear that in mind.

Dangerous consumption

As mentioned at the start, please see your doctor first before withdrawing if you are consuming extremely high volumes of alcohol. Your body will not cope with instant withdrawal. See Appendix I to understand what high levels look like and why it is dangerous to withdraw too quickly.

***

Wellbeing tools

The six streams

If you sit in a dark room and expect change to come, it won't. This is why we need to be considering our wellbeing at the same time along this adventure. A double bonus if you like.

The six streams wellbeing theory is constantly being adapted for different purposes, but the basics are that if you are keeping a number of different wellbeing elements scoring high, then your overall wellbeing will be balanced. It is so easy to ignore looking after ourselves day to day. We might not notice the impact this has on us until one day we are really struggling. We might not understand why because we didn't notice that we hadn't been looking after ourselves. This tool just raises awareness. It keeps you in check. If you are firing on all cylinders from a wellbeing perspective you are going to feel strong as we set off together on the Sober Experience. The bonus here is these six streams stand alone from alcohol so they are an additional boost.

Here are the elements I would love you to look at. The idea is that you rate yourself daily (or as often as you can in the week) from 1 to 10 in each of the elements with 1 being not very strong and 10 being really strong. That way you can pick up when one of the elements starts to dip and you can take action.

Sleep: are you getting that deep restorative sleep that you deserve? Removing the alcohol will massively help that.

Nutrition: water, balanced diet, energy giving foods, pay attention to what you are putting into your body.

Movement: regular movement, be it maximising the moves you make around the house, taking advantage of a quick 2 minutes to do some squats, or regular specific exercise.

Connection: humans need connection – having moments of meaningful connection planned into your week is a huge boost to positivity and wellbeing.

Recovery: life just keeps on coming. It is often tempting to ignore our wellbeing and not take opportunities to recover. Recovery requires a conscious choice to stop and take a break – whatever that looks like to you.

Positivity: each day find time to look for 3 positives, whether in your head or on paper. As we discuss in Lesson 3 and 4 a focus on the positive can be a powerful driver to change.

Sleep	Nutrition	Movement	Connection	Recovery	Positivity
1	1	1	1	1	1
2	2	2	2	2	2
3	3	3	3	3	3
4	4	4	4	4	4
5	5	5	5	5	5
6	6	6	6	6	6
7	7	7	7	7	7
8	8	8	8	8	8
9	9	9	9	9	9
10	10	10	10	10	10

Journaling

I come across so much resistance to journaling. "It's not for me" is often swiftly followed by "but I read about how beneficial it is". I think there is an element of fear that writing down your feelings will trigger you somehow. So here is my suggestion:

Firstly, I really do encourage you to note down the exercises each day in a notebook. To note the positives, to do the check-ins, to set goals, to check in with your six streams. It is really important to do this. It is positive reinforcement.

And then phase two. The journal is a way of checking in. I am not asking you to write out your whole day's experiences or your life story. There is a 5 minute journal template on my website and my technique is to spend that brief time reflecting on any positives, a goal and your values, as many days of the week as you can remember. This can really build on your wellbeing.

There are so many journal books out there to buy. I prefer a cheap notebook. Each day during that first year of my own sobriety I would write in the journal. My positives were around alcohol change. My goal was unrelated, giving me a completely different focus. It kept me positive, grounded and looking ahead. I have gone on and off the boil with journaling over the past four years. I struggle with consistency in everything except my sobriety!, but it was a massive tool in the early days and I really hope it will be a regular habit again one day!

Monthly goal setting

Again in the interests of looking ahead, I would set myself goals each month when I was in the early days of the experience. Having a goal for the month gives you a future anchor point. There is a monthly planner template on my website.

A daily check in

Please keep checking in with the following questions to take you back to the task at hand. We have short memories and where alcohol is concerned, short memories really do open us up to a potential blip, so consider it a theory recap. I would love it if you could do this daily.

1. Have you engaged your human today?
2. What will you say to your chimp if he wants a drink?
3. Do you know where you are on the cycle of change?
4. What one positive change can you make today that you didn't do while drinking?

5. Can you do something for yourself in one of the six streams? Have an open mindset about it. Be creative even.

Potential blocks

Before we set off let's address some potential blocks head on before they trip us up:

Drinking to escape

I want to be upfront about a barrier to success which is all too common and really lingers when it isn't exposed. If you feel like you don't like the life you have right now and are drinking to escape from it the incentive to stop drinking is diminished. But! What if I told you your outlook on life is partly due to the drink. It's a bit of a catch 22 unfortunately. It might not have started that way. The drink may have come after the difficult situation, but the drink is now making life harder. I repeat this in a few sections because it catches so many people out. If you drink regularly alcohol is in your system all the time. You suffer withdrawal as soon as you stop drinking. You suffer mentally with the constant alcohol in your system, since after a drinking episode your brain reduces the happy hormones as it tries to rebalance. So you feel low. So you drink to escape that feeling and it becomes a perpetual cycle until you really see that the alcohol is part of the problem.

Where is the shiny me hiding?

Moving on from this, not drinking doesn't necessarily instantly reveal a newer, shinier, happier you. That might take time or might just not feel possible right now due to your personal circumstances. But that doesn't mean it isn't working. It doesn't mean it isn't doing you the most incredible amount of good. You will be able to cope with life's knocks with so much more strength, and your mental health will not be dragged down further by alcohol. Stopping drinking won't necessarily create your dream life or the shiniest version of yourself. It might just make it easier to move forward. And that is a massive achievement. And when you keep doing it you'll become 'shinier' at the speed that's right for you.

Built in negativity bias

You may have heard this before. We are wired to focus on the negative. A kind of fight or flight situation that goes back to prehistoric human days when focusing on the negative (the potential arrival of a sabre tooth tiger) was actually helpful for survival. It isn't that necessary or helpful in most situations nowadays, but we are still inclined to zone in on the negative: bad news, less favourable parts of the day, gossip. Bad news travels faster, negative memories linger longer.

Except when it comes to alcohol. With alcohol we focus on all of the positive aspects and strategically forget the negatives. We remember the happy times, the happy moments of the evening and forget the hangovers, arguments, ill feeling that may have happened. There is a second unhelpful part to this which I mentioned at the start of the book, and I mention it again because it was a lightbulb moment for me: whilst we are glamourising the alcohol consumption we might also be bringing in that negativity bias to our own lives to support our need to drink. Let me explain. If you tend to drink after a tough day you might create an added element of difficulty to your day to justify the drink. If you drink as a reward for coping with the children all day, you might create stories that amplify the difficulties. You might not even be aware of it. I certainly wasn't. Without even noticing I had created an enormous struggle in my head that I would reward with a drink. Having a daughter with additional needs made it easier to justify. I would play the story in my head which of course would come to pass because I had created the scenario, and I was all set for a regular evening wine session. The trouble is for me, the more I drank the more difficult my life became as the alcohol was really not helping my physical and mental health. And here is where the catch 22 comes into play. The more difficult life became, the more I needed the reward of the drink.

In this section I first ask you to look for any potential blockages that might get in the way of our progress. It really helps to consider potential stumbling blocks at the outset so we can tackle them head on.

Honest answers please

When reading this section I would like you to allow that open mind that we discussed to emerge as this will help you in the next section

---

Action steps and journal prompts

You might be nervous about the chances of success but are you feeling positive about the future life you can create? Or if that feels too daunting, can you picture a regular day without the hangover, without the anxiety, without the pull to drink more? What would you achieve? What new actions, hobbies etc. might you introduce?

This is a really important step. It's important that you aren't just viewing alcohol as something you need to eliminate because it is causing you harm. If you feel this way you will feel a loss when you remove it. In other words, if you are only doing it because you have to, it won't work. It might start out that way of course, and that is absolutely fine, but you have to take it to the next level if you want to see this story change. You have to say to yourself "okay I am here because my drinking is

---

causing me harm, but what am I going to gain from a life without it? This is a huge opportunity."

Start engaging in that positive picture, why it actually might be a brilliant idea to stop, and picture all of the positives that will come as a result. If you are struggling to paint a positive picture, we will cover that in Lesson 4. You are welcome to skip to that now for an initial positivity boost.

If you are not in a great place right now this bit might be trickier, so just take small steps, what small positives might you gain? Try to imagine them even if you can't quite see **you** in the picture just yet. We are just trying to change your mind's perception from escaping from alcohol to what you will gain from the experience.

Are you looking to past events as a reason for current drinking habits?

This is all too common but is something that we need to work on. If you stick with that line of thinking you will struggle to move on because we know "you can't change the past," so thinking about it can lead you to think that you can't then change your present. I feel so much empathy for a person's story, their experiences, their history, but focusing on those experiences will not move you forward in the alcohol free space. It will do the opposite. It will anchor you in a complete justification for drinking. It will glue you to the past, a place where your drinking is welcome. So here I would ask you to focus more on the human chimp concept again. Your human (your logical brain) knows you can't change your past, but your chimp (impulsive and irrational brain) might enjoy referring back to it because it knows if you stay in the past you can continue to drink. I caveat again the potential need for therapy if this bit is too hard. If you do feel there are past situations that you need to come to terms with then this would really help.

Can you picture a "you" who doesn't drink?

Think about that imaginary self. Are you active, an early riser, a productive night owl? Are you going back to school? Are you an avid reader, an avid baker who never had the time before? Are you seeing friends more or making new ones? The list of potential lives is endless. If you are unable to start to imagine a life without alcohol in it, however simple that life might be, it is likely that the element of fear might crop up - again pulling you back to the familiar, the "you" that drinks. Just because it is unwanted by your human doesn't change the fact that it's still the safest option. Our minds crave the familiar, regardless of where that might lead us. I discuss this more in Lesson 2. If we can build that positive picture and bring it to life it will really help to remove that fear.

What is your biggest barrier right now?

I want you to think about this for a moment. If you wanted to stop drinking right now, really genuinely stop, does anything spring to mind as being a barrier to this progress? It might be a partner, the stress of your life right now, fear that you can't do it, worrying that you need it as a crutch, your current living arrangements. Or this might be the moment you realise there really aren't any barriers. Awareness can really help us move forward here and it's great to get it out in the open. We will come back to any barriers when we talk about ambivalence later, but I just want you to acknowledge them if they exist, see them for what they are so they aren't hiding away.

So with the questions above I am asking you to do a little thinking so we can at first recognise those blocks, raise your awareness levels and then welcome in the lessons that follow. This will help place you firmly on the path to success.

Tripping yourself up before you have even begun

There will be a tendency to ignore all the advice in my book and any book you might read. I could say I would be almost disappointed if you didn't at first because quite frankly, ignoring this advice means your brain and mind are functioning "normally." Your brain has stored some fabulous memories around alcohol. It has selective memory. Your short term memory has recollections around some negative experiences but those are going to fade as the days go on. They will be replaced by a feeling that maybe things aren't quite as bad as you made out. You do have a tendency to exaggerate, catastrophise even, so is this one of those times? You have done a few days without making any extreme life changes, maybe you didn't have a drinking problem/habit after all. The feeling of "I really need to stop drinking, it is bad for my health and I really feel like it could become a problem" is replaced with "sure, why not, I will take some time out from regular drinking if everyone else is, but I don't think I need to be dramatic about it". And so without even realising it, you have taken yourself right back to "denial" on the cycle of change - the precontemplation stage. You don't realise it because you are still essentially involved in thinking about not drinking, but your thoughts are already taking you back there. You aren't making the changes required to make the habit change stick, because you have already told yourself it isn't really a habit.

But that's just it, it had moved away from being a habit anyway. It had become addictive as we were continuing to do it when we knew it was harming us. Because it is a drug our brains will crave the dopamine hit, the memory will have created those pain reward connections and the next time a situation triggers those you will want to drink.

So don't let your mind trick you into thinking you are fine and don't need to do anything. If you really are fine then what a huge bonus - your new life awaits! but can you just humour me for a few weeks and keep reading. Isn't it worth it just in case? You wouldn't want an aircraft to take off with only the basic checks. So humour me and let's do a more thorough review so we definitely land safely!

It's just too hard

Following on from my previous point, there will be a tendency to then think this is just too hard. But it feels too hard because you had already taken yourself back to denial and you haven't done anything to change that. This change will involve a complete mindset shift so if you haven't done any of the shifting it will indeed feel unachievable!

Fear is more powerful than pleasure

The fear of loss for most people is more powerful than the desire for gain. This is called the Pleasure Pain principle (5). That story that we have built up in our heads creates fear, the story that we need alcohol as a crutch. This is why we need to constantly remap our thinking process to remove that fear.

Limiting beliefs

You may have a number of stories that you tell yourself that are blocking your progress here. "I am not good enough," "I am not strong enough", "I won't cope without alcohol". Such beliefs are just a defence mechanism. Again, it is the fear speaking out trying to protect you. We will work through this in later chapters.

Everything before this point has been crucial learning: the theories, my story, the preparation. The next phase will not land without the ground work. If you would prefer to go back and read Parts I and II again at this point then please do.

The next few parts of the book take you through the Ten Lessons. The idea is that you build: build in knowledge and understanding, build in confidence, build in positivity, build a picture of where you want to get to. The Sober Experience combines the learning up to now and the ten lessons that follow: gaining the knowledge and then using it to follow through with the experience. Please take it at your pace.

Part III

Awareness

The first two lessons start the awareness piece as we look at the brain and mind. They are crucial to laying the foundations of the Sober Experience as the brain and mind control the drinking habit, so we need to understand how they work.

Lesson 1

Understanding the link between alcohol and your brain

> The brain is the organ inside the head that controls thought, memory, feelings and activity.

Having an understanding of what drugs do to our brains is vital, I believe, if you then want to start allowing your mind to tell a different story. It's important to become aware of how powerful drugs are and how complicated the brain is in response to what it perceives to be a foreign substance in the body.

Your body adjusts to anything you put into it. Alcohol changes the levels of certain neurotransmitters (chemical messengers) in the brain and your brain first tries to remove those to rebalance itself (creating next day lows) and then over time, realising there is a regular pattern to the consumption, it adapts and normalises itself at this new level – creating dependency.

The happy hormones

Alcohol changes your brain chemistry. When alcohol enters the bloodstream, it also affects the nervous system, and brain cells and causes brain functions to produce more happy hormones - neurotransmitters such as serotonin and dopamine.

Serotonin is used by the brain to enable normal behavioural functions such as eating and sleeping. It makes you feel calm.

Dopamine is your reward system. It makes you feel pleasure, satisfaction, and motivation. Dopamine also encourages you to repeat the same action in the future as your brain perceives it as a good thing and as something that is helping you. Dopamine impacts memory as, through evolution, the brain has had to build memories of what it perceives as "helpful" to survival.

Imagine that when you drink alcohol your brain is flooded with these happy chemical messengers. Basically, serotonin, the mood regulator and dopamine, the mood booster. So, in the moment you can essentially feel happier when you drink alcohol.

So addictive substances, such as alcohol, hijack our natural reward system, and this can lead to the cycle of dependence as your brain continues to seek that same pleasurable feeling.

Tolerance

All addictive drugs produce dopamine. They cause dopamine to flood the reward pathway ten times higher than a natural reward would. Over chronic use nothing natural will compare and through regular and increasing substance use, the brain circuits adapt and reduce their sensitivity to dopamine, so you need more to get the same effect. This is called tolerance: because the brain is being flooded with dopamine constantly it adapts and actually reduces the number of dopamine receptors, releasing less dopamine so you have to drink more to get the same effect.

GABA

Alcohol makes you feel relaxed: it tampers with the parts of your brain that make you more active and that is why you might feel more relaxed after a drink. This is because alcohol increases the production of a chemical messenger called GABA which is an inhibitory neurotransmitter, inhibitory effectively meaning slowing you down. This makes you think more slowly which can stop you feeling nervous among other things. It essentially dulls your senses which can feel useful in a stress inducing situation - new crowd of people, if you are naturally nervous, wanting to relax after a long day etc. It seemingly has many "benefits". The downside of GABA is it slows down your ability to function in a number of ways:

GABA slows down your thought processes, so it becomes harder to make decisions.

GABA slows down your brain communications affecting movement which can make you clumsy. The more you drink the clumsier you get.

GABA inhibits your awareness so you might put yourself in dangerous situations.

GABA can make you mis-read facial expressions and gestures so you might think someone is angry when they aren't at all. This is why you often see increased tension in high alcohol consuming environments.

Glutamate

We have seen that alcohol increases the inhibitory neurotransmitter GABA. Well, it also represses an excitatory neurotransmitter, glutamate. Excitatory neurotransmitters encourage a cell to take action. By inhibiting these cells, we are effectively slowing down. This accounts for the "depressant" effect of alcohol. We discuss later how, as your body attempts to re-balance you, you may feel low the next day, but the actual "depressing" element of alcohol is this - it depresses i.e. weakens/lowers your excitatory neurotransmitters. This leads to the slowing down of parts of the brain – affecting inhibition control, thought, perception, attention, judgement, memory, sleep, and co-ordination, and these become more impaired as consumption increases. Even incredibly low levels of alcohol can have an impact on glutamate.

Raising your baseline

It's important to know that your brain adapts to any chemical that enters your bloodstream. It first tries to reject the alcohol: if you drink more than your body can cope with it might trigger you to vomit as a rescue reflex. But in continuing to drink regularly your brain adjusts by reducing the number of receptors that allow the chemicals in. What this means in terms of your body's response to alcohol is that you become used to life with that volume of alcohol in your system. Your brain has adapted, so the level of alcohol consumption is now the norm. Because the brain is trying to control how many chemicals it releases, you will need more to get the same effect. Your baseline essentially raises. You build up a tolerance and need more for the same boost.

Symptoms of excessive drinking

Extremes of emotion

I have explained how alcohol lowers your inhibitions via the neurotransmitter (GABA) and depresses your excitatory control (glutamate). This can have an enormous impact on your mood and your emotions in one sitting if you continue in a drinking "session".

The impact that GABA has on your control, thoughts, perception, and judgement can have a significant negative impact. Let's bring our human and chimp back into play. As you drink more in an evening (with our human knowing we can only process one unit an hour – see appendix I, but our chimp not caring) the impact on GABA and glutamate becomes problematic. Alcohol depresses the ability to regulate emotion which is why we can often become emotional or aggressive when drunk. Because your problem solving and decision-making abilities have become impaired, it can feel at the time like anger or other sudden outbursts of upset are the only option.

Your impaired judgement may cause you to mis-read situations, signs, faces, and be less conscious about getting into an argument. If you bump into someone in a bar, when sober you would think nothing of it. When drunk you may perceive it as a deliberate act of aggression. As I said, we find it much harder to read the true emotion on a person's face when drunk.

This is such a critical area to consider during this experience. The very messengers that make you feel good at the outset continue sending the same messages, but as the volume increases the impact they are having starts to become negative and therefore not the desired effect you were initially seeking.

Hangover

A hangover is the result of drinking to excess. Even one drink can interrupt the natural cycles of sleep, causing a nervous or irritable feeling the next morning. This is one of the symptoms of a hangover.

Other symptoms of a hangover are dizziness, the shakes, numb feelings - these are all due to the low blood sugar levels caused by alcohol. This can lead to feelings of anxiety.

Another cause of the hangover is the additional chemicals that are introduced to alcohol during production - the sulphates put into wine as a preservative can induce headaches for example.

Alcohol consumption also leads to dehydration. It is a fairly strong diuretic, meaning it causes the body to lose water by increasing the frequency of trips to the toilet. Dehydration also causes the fatigue and weaknesses discussed above - some of these symptoms are mimicking the feeling of anxiety which brings us on to **hangxiety.**

Hangxiety

This is the term that brings together a regular hangover and resulting anxiety. The feeling of anxiety is caused by the low levels of GABA as your body tries to rebalance the excess. When GABA is low you are more prone to anxious thoughts. Combine that with the physical symptoms of dehydration, and tiredness from the disruption to our sleep. The other cause of hangxiety is the memory blackouts.

Hangovers will in theory get worse with age as it takes your body longer to process the alcohol. With increased age our bodies tend to have a higher fat proportion. Body fat absorbs the alcohol making it hard for the liver enzymes to expel from the body.

Whenever you have a craving consider the feelings of hangxiety and hangovers - it might make you think twice. These are the reality of drinking to excess. These experiences are the ones we conveniently forget.

Blackouts

"A black out is a period of alcohol induced amnesia which typically happens at high blood alcohol levels. Gaps appear in a person's memory when a person drinks enough alcohol to temporarily block the transfer of memories from short-term to long-term storage - known as memory consolidation - in a brain area called the hippocampus." (1) Blackouts are more likely to occur when alcohol enters the bloodstream quickly - if someone drinks on an empty stomach or drinks a lot in a short space of time.

Blackouts are not the same as passing out. In a blackout you are still awake - you are just not converting experiences to memories. With passing out you actually fall asleep or lose consciousness from drinking too much.

Rebalance of neurotransmitters

The negative impact of the happy hormone boost is more likely to happen the next day. Because you are artificially boosting these levels, your body steps in by trying to balance out the chemicals, so the next day you will actually feel a comparative deficit in these chemicals which can often lead to you feeling low. This accounts for the common misconception that it is a depressant (that and the possible inability to control your emotions during the night causing potential outbursts of emotion). So, the following morning, as the happy hormones rebalance themselves, your mood will dip.

Hair of the dog

Withdrawal. If you have a regular drinking habit that feeling the next day is partly due to withdrawal. That was a frightening realisation for me. When you wake up and your hangover is so severe, part of that is due to your drinking volume being so significant that your body has gone into withdrawal and craves another drink. We joke about it, but the reality is a bit worrying. Having another drink is just feeding the withdrawal. Where your body has normalised alcohol consumption it actually craves the alcohol to feel balanced.

So why look at the brain when we are discussing alcohol? As I said, I believe society creates a very biased view of alcohol. I want you to have all the facts.

Impacting other parts of the body

Alcohol consumption leads to stomach problems - alcohol releases acid which can irritate the lining of the stomach.

Acetaldehyde - a toxic bi-product of alcohol metabolism - contributes to inflammation of the liver, pancreas, brain, and other organs.

The danger of instant withdrawal

Alcohol is consumed. On consumption it hits your bloodstream instantly and your brain in minutes. Alcohol is a small molecule and as such it can travel easily throughout the entire body. It has unpredictable results because of its size, and the fact it can attach itself to the neurotransmitters in the body in different ways. So, it is different for everyone as you may well have noticed already.

Alcohol is physically addictive. In fact, it is so physically addictive that it is one of the only drugs that withdrawing from it suddenly can actually kill you when consumption is significant: all drugs change the brain chemistry, but if your consumption is at an extreme level, removing it suddenly will cause a huge deficit in certain neurotransmitters and your brain might go into shutdown. This is why I always place caution over plans to change your relationship with alcohol. If your drinking is at higher levels, you will need doctor supervision to withdraw and you will need to do it gradually at first. See the section on units of alcohol in the Appendix I.

ACTION STEPS AND JOURNAL PROMPTS

1. Reflect on the information in this chapter. Which parts resonate with you?

2. Write in your journal about any thoughts and experiences you've had that connect with what you've just learned about the ways in which alcohol can affect your brain.

3. Read the section on units of alcohol in Appendix I and consider discussing your plans to lower your alcohol intake with your doctor. If your alcohol intake has been high, you should take medical guidance on reducing and stopping your alcohol consumption.

Lesson 2

How to change your mindset around alcohol

What makes one person succeed in giving up drinking and another struggle has a lot to do with the mind games. I can't change the situation you are in, but I can help you change the mindset. Alcohol has simply become your mind's response to different situations in life.

The chimp likes a drink

I introduced you to the chimp in Part I, but now let's relate the concept to alcohol. Your human mind, the part of your mind that thinks logically, has had a thought: It would like to consider drinking less or even nothing at all.

That instant perception of giving up alcohol is one of struggle, difficulty (immediately the negative concerns that we will discuss in Lesson 3). You may have already tried it and been unsuccessful. You may have seen others struggle. Society is sending so many messages that this is not going to be an easy task. There is nothing about this that is screaming "a walk in the park." So, this brings us to the bit in the middle. The resistance. This consists of your thoughts, the stories you have saved to memory about the past and present, the perception of the future, the world that you have created with alcohol in it. It isn't the actual pictures and memories that cause the block, it's your manipulation and perception of them.

The future hasn't happened yet. You have no idea if you will struggle to give up alcohol, but your perception is that you will. So how do we address this? Well firstly we go back to the human and chimp concept. We need to work on our thoughts and responses.

- My thoughts associated with alcohol were that I deserved it as a reward for the many roles I had.

- Your chimp will impulsively tell you to just go on and have a drink.

- Your chimp will become agitated with some unwelcome news or feeling let down in some way and think you deserve a drink to make it better. This is called "**drinking on a feeling.**"

- Your chimp will encourage you to have more than you wanted to drink because your chimp is impulsive and "in the moment" - he doesn't think ahead to future consequences of his actions.

- Your chimp will say you are boring without a drink.

- Your chimp will say you need a drink for confidence.

- Your chimp will tell you it's all just too hard and you won't succeed.

Appeasing the chimp

By being aware of the presence of our chimp we can learn to engage our human to challenge him.

Our human knows alcohol isn't the solution, that we had planned to manage our drinking, and we don't want another one, that our upset is probably not as bad as our chimp thinks and alcohol certainly won't improve it.

Our human can retrieve the correct program from the computer and calm the chimp down. If we are acknowledging that our chimp is talking, we can get the computer on board.

Our human cares about our overall well-being and knows that we won't feel good after drinking.

Our human knows everything outside of that moment of drinking will end up being harder to cope with if we are hungover.

Our human knows we are exaggerating the benefits of alcohol and ignoring the negatives.

Action steps and journal prompts

In any situation where you risk compromising your drinking goal:

Ask yourself who is talking: your human or your chimp?

Ask yourself "do I want to feel like this?"

Accept that your chimp is alerting you to a problem that needs a solution - so if it thinks it needs a drink find something else for it to do - it may well be bored, it may need connection. Do something. Act on the alert by doing anything other than drinking.

Remind yourself that you have a choice to operate in either of the three systems: human, chimp, or computer. Don't stay in chimp mode where you are vulnerable.

In the short-term try to avoid known situations when the chimp might pop up.

The stories we tell ourselves

Think about what language you are using when you think you need a drink. Again let's talk about the chimp. If you think you **need** a drink, is it your human or your chimp talking? What would you advise a friend who said they **needed it** when you know they were trying to stop?

There will **always** be a reason to drink. Society is designed that way. We must get that point out there right now. This is probably the biggest area where people slip up. When your energy reserves are low, your reasons to **not** drink start to fade, the desire to drink can start creeping back and you will seek **the reason,** any reason, and a reason will **always** be there because we live in a society that encourages drinking.

By owning that right now you can begin to arm yourself with that counter-argument. Engage your human mind. Pull back to those reasons you have for reducing your alcohol consumption. Tell yourself that this too shall pass. A craving is momentary. Play it forward - an exercise we will discuss later.

Action steps and journal prompts

1. Challenge your chimp's suggestion when it says you "need or deserve a drink".

2. Do you really? What does that really mean? What is your chimp trying to tell you? What is the feeling that you are trying to enhance or avoid?

3. What can you do instead? And if it is too late this time, then really think about it and get those plans in place for next time.

Catastrophizing

> To think about the worst things that could possibly happen in a situation, or to consider a situation as much worse or much more serious than it really is

In line with the reasons to drink, catastrophizing can often lead us down a rabbit hole which often ends in "needing a drink", so here we are combining the language that we use around alcohol with creating reasons to drink by projecting irrational worries from our Chimp mind. So, all the learnings come crashing together here in this most energy draining of activities. Treating chronic catastrophizing can be done with Cognitive Behavioural Therapy (CBT), but for our purposes we simply want to acknowledge mild catastrophizing and make some effort to prevent it.

Action steps and journal prompts

- Ask yourself who is talking, your human or your chimp?

- Try to bring yourself back to the present moment.

- Ask yourself is this thought helpful?

- Celebrate that catastrophizing often means you care, but realise you are burning energy that you could be using for more productive activities in this moment.

> • Write it out - write down what is worrying you and score
> it on a scale of 1-10 and write out the possible causes of
> your worry. If you do this exercise, the occasions where you
> catastrophize will become less, and most often you won't
> find a concrete reason for the catastrophizing.

Socialising sober – common misconceptions

There are a lot of misconceptions where alcohol is concerned – those mind
tricks that keep the dream alive and the charade centre stage.

Am I missing out? This can make you feel so uncomfortable in the early
days until you get a handle on your chimp. Other people's laughter and
gestures are often magnified when you first experience an outing sober.
Socialising sober is deemed hardcore - not for the fainthearted, well this was
my interpretation anyway. For some people during those initial outings, the
fun (that you feel you aren't having) is unbearable! This is all your chimp
talking. You have probably been worrying about the outing long before
embarking on it, so had been anticipating a difficult ride - again going in
with that negative mindset therefore engineering a negative experience. So,
let's pause and let's engage our human. How can it possibly be that hard?
You are still out with your friends, hearing the same stories, engaging with
people, experiencing the same atmosphere, all that is missing is the alcohol.
You just have to reassure your chimp that this is the case. It might be
unfamiliar, but it doesn't have to be unpleasant. So, engage your human's
rational thoughts at times like this to calm your chimp.

There is of course another side to being out and trying not drinking - the
fact that you might be triggered, and if you feel outings might be triggering

at first then it is important to change the way you connect for a while – see Lesson 5.

Everyone will notice me not drinking: It is a common human trait when we do something outside our comfort zone that we feel everyone notices. In the sober circles I mix in, yes there is the odd story where someone has felt really uncomfortable on a night out as they have been called out on their not drinking and encouraged to have one. But this is rare. Because the fact is most people don't notice and don't care. Contrary to what your chimp might be telling you, you aren't walking around with an enormous sign on your head telling everyone this big news, and it just isn't big news to most people.

I do chuckle now when I think about my response when people asked me what I wanted to drink. It was such a massive question for me, but to the person asking the question it was of course just routine. "I don't drink," "I have stopped drinking," squirming in my seat, desperately scouring the menu for the alcohol-free options, cursing when I couldn't find any. Now I am far more relaxed of course. Everything just takes time. In the early days you might feel more reassured to plan what you might have to drink beforehand and even look at the drinks menu online so you know what your options are.

Everyone else will be drinking: I am sure you have experienced that feeling. Because you have always associated a good night out with drinking, you assume everyone else would of course be drinking. It was astonishing for me to realise that there are actually a lot of us that don't feel the need to drink on nights out, or to just stop at one or two. We come back to the chimp. Your chimp is telling you that everyone else will be drinking, that you are abandoning the tribe, that you will no longer fit in. But the second you start experiencing non-drinking nights out you will notice how many other people are doing it too! You see what you want to see, and in the past, you have gravitated towards the drinking folk. You simply didn't notice everyone else. Now open your eyes and look around. The big reveal! Not everyone does actually drink all the time!

Alcohol gives me confidence: This is an absolute classic reason people associate with drinking. I always thought it too: "alcohol gives me much needed confidence" - that "confidence" you think you have is your brain being flooded with an increase in GABA (discussed in Lesson 1) so your inhibitions are reduced, and your mind becomes fogged. That is it. You basically care less so feel more confident. But imagine the confidence you would get from being fully connected to your surroundings - the opposite of what alcohol does. Imagine the confidence you might gain from being fully able to listen when you are with your friends, to fully appreciate what is around you. It can feel alien at first. You feel like you have a label on your head identifying you as being different, but you really don't, and you really aren't different. That is just your chimp trying to rattle you. The confidence also comes from coming out of your comfort zone. Something amazing happens when you begin to change your relationship with alcohol in that you start to try other new things. The blinkers on life are lifted - I mention this at length in the introduction to the book if you missed it. Anything becomes possible when you go against the grain of society and find that you have a newfound desire to experiment and explore.

I am boring without it: This is such an interesting concept and a really common worry for people. So why do we genuinely feel boring without alcohol at first?

Advertising – alcohol is perceived to be fun, a relaxant, a party starter. It is all in the marketing – so you have been targeted to feel this way.

New stimulation required - for the last few years you have been accustomed to essentially numbing your brain for pleasure and now, with less alcohol in your system, your brain is looking for more stimulation. Work with this. That feeling of boring/boredom will lessen with all the other work we are doing around changing your lifestyle.

Brain – we discussed how alcohol artificially boosts those happy hormones in our brain at levels much higher than we could naturally produce them –and so reducing those will have a seemingly negative effect in the very short term as our natural rewards will take time to fill the gap. You must remember it is short term though. Chemical highs including alcohol produce instant gratification. The buzz from drinking happens quickly. It takes time for your brain to adjust to accepting delayed forms of gratification - those natural rewards from your natural environment, but they will come.

Open your mind. This is where the fun begins

For so many reasons a life with excess alcohol in it has narrowed your field of vision. As I have mentioned in the other sections, if we have been leading a life with this alcohol habit heavily embedded in it, we have had to cut back on other life elements in order to sustain it. It happens over a long period of time, so you have probably barely noticed it. By diminishing your life, alcohol has left you with nothing else to hold on to.

Action steps and journal prompts

Challenge your chimp's suggestion when it says you are boring with-out it. Enter into human mode as you question:

- Are you more able to likely to engage with what's going on?

- Are you more in control of your behaviour throughout the evening?

- Are you more authentic? – being yourself rather than a numbed version of you.

- Will you remember far more of the evening?

Give yourself time to adjust to a you that isn't numbed by alcohol.

Things to watch out for

Living on autopilot

Ticking all the boxes, not upsetting anyone but not setting the world alight. It is just so easy to go with the flow. Our minds have less thinking to do when we go through the same motions we always have. But what if you actually do stop and think? That is what this book is all about. You have already paused for thought just by being here, so you are disrupting that autopilot mechanism. It is worth noting the existence of autopilot and calling it out for what it is - an unconscious default that allows you to get on with things without much thought, but in the case of alcohol, a risky path that can lead to a familiar but unwanted habit. Autopilot might lead you to a drink before you have even noticed so we need to avoid using autopilot in those early weeks. We need to be operating with conscious thought.

The f*ck it button override

What is the 'f*ck it button? It's when you're in a situation - maybe one that's difficult emotionally, or one where you're having fun, and your chimp confuses that with needing a drink - and return to drinking. It's important that you are honest with yourself here. I can most often tell when a client has pressed the button. They have lost focus on me, and they might start to engage in thoughts of the past. They are volunteering a stream of negative feelings and despite their best efforts, they have no real interest in my words of support (the nods and murmurs don't fool me). The excuses are coming thick and fast, the justifications are placing them right back in their comfort zone ensuring their next move is a drink. They have gone into panic mode.

If you arrive at this point it is very difficult to come back from it at that moment. It was actually to address the f*ck it button that I wrote this book. Because when a client presses it there is usually radio silence for a time, and I can't reach them. With this book I can reach you and I urge you to pick the book up the next day and jump back in. There is no shame, no guilt. This is simply a process, it's all part of the experience.

So how to avoid pressing the button? You either tackle this head on before it happens, when you are in a good space, or you hope like hell you are in for calm seas. The latter scenario is unlikely as life is never easy all the time, and even if it was, there is another issue we must consider. If there is the slightest of triggers, however mild, your mind will lead you down a negative path anyway as it knows it's the fastest way to a drink. So even if life is generally calm, in those early days, your mind might seek out the negatives and elaborate them to bring you back to the familiar place of drinking.

So, we need to disarm the f*ck it button for good, and if it's a powerful one with a bit of a loose connection we need to prioritise this. If you have been stuck in a loop using the term (which I have banned with clients) "day 1" then you are constantly on a negative trajectory, you are seeing it as a battle, and battles sound like effort, and we often tend to avoid effort by sabotaging it.

Action steps and journal prompts

- What do you need to tell yourself to believe you deserve a future with more energy?

- What thoughts do you need to let go of to prevent this sabotage?

- What thoughts are you telling yourself that are leading to drink?

- Who is talking when you are saying these words? Your human or your chimp? This is a rhetorical question. We both know it's your chimp. Your human has made the practical acknowledgement that alcohol isn't good for you. So, it must be your chimp?

- If you are creating a negative future picture we need to bring you back to the present. The future is unknown, but it will be dealt with much, much better sober. That is a fact. A fact that your human knows fully but your chimp needs to be convinced.

- What one step can you take right now? And then repeat this. Each step will give you strength.

Yes, life may be tricky, but drinking WILL NOT HELP. Don't drink just because you don't have the answers and as I keep saying, your mind may well have enlarged any current problems to give you permission to drink. So, it's not the problem that is the problem, it's the drink habit. Don't confuse the two.

- What are you afraid of? We fear the unknown and a life without alcohol is unknown. So, what exactly are you afraid of? Anxiety, self-doubt, shame? These are all symptoms of increased alcohol consumption. Please know that there is nothing to fear. It just requires you to give it a try, to take the first step.

There is one other dimension to this button where I challenge its effect. Let's consider the point I made about it being really difficult to come back from once you have decided to press it. What if something were actually to happen to trigger the sudden need for an alternative direction, for a recall of that button pressing: an accident with the need for a sudden admittance to hospital, the last-minute offer of a trip to the Caribbean requiring you to leave right now (unlikely I know), an issue with a family member involving your complete attention! A lightning bolt of positivity, or a sudden change in state requiring medical attention and the transportation to a place that you don't associate with alcohol - hospital - will change your state. It will change the trajectory of your negative thought pattern. It will jolt you out of that moment. So that means it isn't written in stone. We could disarm the button in the moment, but **WE** choose not to, and we have to own that and ask ourselves is it because we are....

Drinking to not feel?

We drink to block a feeling or emotion. It is a coping mechanism. So, without that crutch how do we deal with that feeling or emotion? People often find it difficult to feel the feelings so entirely at first, but they realise quite quickly that the whole emotional experience is easier to tolerate without alcohol - that numbing comes at such a price.

Action steps and journal prompts

Again, journaling can be a great tool to explore and work through the feelings. Writing out those thoughts. Digging deeper and questioning those feelings can start to create a positive shift.

Breathing is another tool that can change our state. It calms the nervous system, and it can balance your mood. It can lower your blood pressure and heart rate which reduces the stress hormones in your blood. There are many free breathing meditations and exercises that can be found online.

Looking at the six streams - working on strengthening your overall wellbeing will again support your ability to cope with different emotions.

Give it time. It's new so try to feel the feelings, knowing that the overall situation will be so much easier without the alcohol.

Taking all these positive steps will help raise your bar, a concept that I talk about in Lesson 9 - the level you fall to when a difficult situation occurs. Doing all these things combined with not drinking will contribute much further to raising that bar.

Part IV

Positivity

These next two lessons look at positivity. The Sober Experience is a positive one but we might not always see that so these two lessons will help raise those positivity levels.

Lesson 3

Building a story around the statement

How can you really want to get somewhere if you don't know where somewhere is? If you don't know what somewhere looks like, feels like, sounds like? You might know you need to make a change, and you might put your best efforts into it at the beginning but memories fade and the reasons you initially had for not drinking might become weaker. So, let's create a home for this desire to stop drinking. If we don't know what it might look like we won't know what we are aiming for.

Turning the statement into a story

You are thinking about stopping drinking. That is a statement. I ask you, what's the story behind it? This is a step that you will need to go back and re-visit and strengthen at times. As we have already learnt, the mind is powerful, so we need to build a really powerful story around this, something for both your human AND your chimp to latch on to. Let's not forget alcohol is addictive and humans don't naturally like change. We fear the unknown (as mentioned) so logically we need to create a comfortable and enticing home for this statement of "I want to stop drinking." Let's think about that for a moment.

Action steps and journal prompts

What will it feel like to have your evenings back? An evening where you have mental control, where you aren't feeling pressured into a habit, where you don't then feel guilty for succumbing to the habit.

What will it feel like to go to bed sober? To end the day when you want to at the right time for you and feeling strong.

What will it feel like to wake up with a clear, fresh head? How would you start your day? How much would you achieve first thing in the morning if you choose to?

What will you do with the extra energy? You won't have all the answers as such. You might not have experienced a life without alcohol in a very long time - maybe even ever in your adult life but use your imagination and dig deep.

Think about the six streams. What other elements can you think of? Challenge yourself. The more inviting the story, the more you will want to live it!

You might not feel in a position to do this right now and that's okay. It's okay to read this book through and maybe you will start to pick up on the positive energy later on. Then you can come back to this point.

Potential barriers to the positivity step

Fearing the unknown

Let's just be realistic. As I said, you probably haven't experienced sober life for a very long time. The picture is unknown, and it is really common that we fear the unknown because we have no information, so our brain doesn't know how to cope. It doesn't know what it is looking for and can't see a clear path ahead. But it's important we recognise this fear as then we can support it. If we don't address this from the outset then as soon as our brain realises it is going down a path it doesn't recognise it is going to panic, and how do we often deal with panic? If you are in that loop right now because it is a loop, then please keep reading as the knowledge gained will help push you forward.

It is the fear of the unknown that might make building a positive story tricky. But try as hard as you can as this is such an important step.

Tunnel vision

I can't stress this point enough that is why I do repeat it. Drinking alcohol might well have been heavily embedded in your life for years. It will have taken a physical and mental toll over that time and, to cope with the added weight, your vision of your life may well be narrowed. As I mentioned earlier you may be coping with life, but your life will have shrunk to enable you to manage. So building a story around giving up alcohol might be a step you need to re-visit after you have spent a few days working on those six streams. If right now you are sitting in the dark room and really can't see how to widen that lens, then take just one element from the six streams exercise and then come back to this lesson. If you can take even just small daily steps you will start to move forward.

Lesson 4

Creating a positive picture of a life without alcohol

We need to create a picture that is positive. The outcome of this change - removing the alcohol - needs to feel like a positive one for it to stick.

a) Let's use the right language here

Think about it. If you use the right language, adopt the right game face, walk with the confidence of someone who means business, then you will naturally feel stronger in living this Sober Experience. Positivity breeds positivity. Positivity attracts positivity pure and simple. So what do I mean by this in terms of language?

Firstly: you are evolving: When I think about the encounters I have had with excessive alcohol consumption throughout my life there is so much negativity, sadness, darkness, struggle. Yet when I looked at stopping there was also negativity surrounding what not drinking would look like. Words like teetotal, problem, abstinence seemed to dominate. Even the word recovery, which connects some individuals, puts some people off seeking support. It can feel too permanent. Yet when I decided to stop drinking there was only light, positive energy, encouragement. Not because everything turned out brilliantly every day. Of course it didn't. Not because it was easy and success (which for me was stopping altogether) happened on the first try for me. It didn't. Giving up alcohol isn't a golden ticket to the dream life, it's the golden ticket to losing a cloud that was hovering over your life without you even realising it. It's a ticket to removing the blinkers you didn't know were there. It's a ticket to viewing life from a different perspective. This is why I don't think you should focus on any feeling of a permanent struggle even if it feels like that initially. Quite the opposite. As I said, you are evolving.

Day 1, we go again, back to it: how can it be day 1 unless it really is the very first day? Feeling like you are constantly going backwards, constantly having to repeat the process from the very beginning, just isn't positive for your mindset so try not to say it.

I HAVE to stop: Here there is a sense of desperation. You can't carry on like this. I get that, but you need to switch it to the positive. What will you gain from the experience? I want you to want to stop because of all of the gains. As I said before, so often those seemingly powerful reasons to stop that are based on a negative, fade away.

I don't want to feel like this: what **do** you want to feel like? If you keep focusing on what you don't want to feel like your subconscious mind will take you there anyway because it's on your mind.

Don't keep focusing on what might have been: so, you wish you hadn't had that drink. You wish you hadn't wasted so much time. You wish you had tried this years ago. It isn't helpful to reflect on what you can't change, apart from to take the positives about what you will change. Allowing your mind to focus on negatives is just fuelling the part of you that uses drink to numb pain.

Groundhog day: just saying the words fills me with a sense of exasperation. Yes, if you have been doing this for some time now you might feel inclined to use that analogy, but let's try not to. You have done this before so what will you do differently? How will it absolutely not be like Groundhog Day? What have you learnt that you can use to take you further next time?

b) Don't base the decision on a negative event

If you embark upon this experience on the back of a hangover, on the back of a terrible drinking episode you are leaping in with negative thinking, with a reactive not proactive brain. It will work of course, but only for a few days. Why? Because you won't physically want to drink for a few days anyway because of the hangover. The guilt might carry you another few days. Willpower might hop on too and take you another few days. You could make very little effort and manage a brief stint. But do not be fooled. After a short period, some distance starts to form between the initial desire to stop. When the memory starts to fade from that start point, when our mind starts to edit some of the details, to soften the impact, to lose some of the emotion, when the hangover subsides, this is when alcohol will start to come back into focus.

c) Be aware that conviction might fade

Actually, this wasn't so important after all. That burning conviction when your head is banging and the memory of you falling down the stairs is both physically present in the bruises and painfully burned on your memory that sits within your throbbing head. Roll forward a few days. Not so important now. How many times have we said or heard someone say, "I am never drinking again," only to do that very thing at the next opportunity. It is the most meaningless statement that I have certainly said at times. Is that our subconscious desire? A cry for help from our battered body and mind? Please stop doing this to me! There must be something in it because it is a pretty common thing to say, and we really mean it in that instant, and then it passes.

d) Catch 22

The thing with alcohol is that we so often use it as a reward/justification for a bad experience. This was a penny drop moment for me. Excessive drinking can make you feel so lousy, it blinkers your view of life, it exaggerates your life problems as it detaches you from reality and depresses your logical thought patterns. The hangover depletes your energy. The guilt plagues your thoughts. You can feel so lousy in fact that you need a drink to curb all of those feelings, and so the cycle begins. You basically need a drink to get over the physical and mental impact of a drinking session.

e) Is it because you can't, or you don't want to?

Again, really think about it. Are you telling yourself you want to stop, or does your body and mind right now feel like it just can't drink? If it's the latter that is driving this then that just won't last: That physical feeling, that unpleasant memory will not last.

Action steps and journal prompts

Let's engage that positivity. The hangover i.e. the negative experience, might well be a wakeup call. But then let's engage our logical human brain. Think about why giving up alcohol will be good for ME, and this goes back to Lesson 3.

Reflecting each day on a positive is crucial to keeping you on the right trajectory. I ask you to note down at least one positive each day from not drinking. Whether you physically write this down and incorporate

---

it with the suggested journaling or think it in your head. Just do a check in each day with the positives you have gained.

Reflecting on my own negative pattern

The memories of those negative events do form part of the story, but further down the line. I now reflect back on some of the many drinking nights and have come to realise I didn't need the alcohol. I have done a lot of reflection on myself and where I was at the time, whether the struggling mum or traumatised teen. I realise I never stopped to find an alternative remedy or to really reflect on the price of those few hours of sedation. I can see so clearly now how my mind cleverly distorted the memories of those heavy drinking nights so that I just kept repeating them. Yes, life has its challenges, but in my previous drinking life I literally expected to drink when anything negative happened. That was the standard path, a complete habit loop - problem followed by drink to numb it. I just forgot to properly appraise the situation and realise that it actually never helped.

Action steps and journal prompts

Be aware your mind may well try to sabotage this process. It will throw problems at you in an effort to allow you to justify drinking. That isn't to deny that there has been a problem, but wanting a drink also pushes you to create problems or worsen problems to enable you to achieve the end goal. Just remember to re-engage your human at this point.

We are all different. We come to this point with a different history consisting of our own interpretation of events up to this point. We might feel broken in parts. We might feel blessed but simply have unwittingly allowed the habit of drinking in. Either way, alcohol is highly addictive, and we are here now with an unwanted habit of excessively drinking it. I want you to work on not getting stuck in the loop, really work on how to avoid this whether we call it catch 22 or Groundhog day as I have described, this LOOP is the repetitive scenario that only changes when something changes, when you change something to break the cycle.

This is a lesson that you might want to come back to.

CHECKPOINT

"TO PLANT A GARDEN IS TO BELIEVE IN

TOMORROW" Audrey Hepburn

Are you ready to plant a garden? I came across the quote while writing the book, and, whilst at first glance it might appear a little left field for this kind of book, I instantly connected with it and its relevance to the Sober Experience. I believe it is a real indicator of where your mind is at. Are you at the point where you could plant a garden? Do you have confidence that the little steps you take now will create positive future change, future growth? Do you believe in your ability to keep the garden growing? You may well not be there yet, but you can keep repeating certain steps - **the mind section, the six streams, the positivity section.** We need to have confidence in this to move to the next lesson.

You drink because it's become a habit: your way of responding to situations, thoughts, events, a coping mechanism. We have learnt how powerful and committed to drinking our society is. We know we want to stop, but we might not believe in an alcohol-free tomorrow yet - the tomorrow where we are thriving. We don't believe that if we planted a seed now, that we are going to commit to watering it. We might not yet have confidence that it's going to grow.

Don't feel disheartened at all at this point. I just want you to engage honestly about where your head is at. Because when we struggle through this experience it is just learning, and a sign that we need to do a little more work.

So, let's get back to the bottom line. If you are not at the garden growing stage yet, answer this question "Do you want change?"

If the answer is yes, please take yourself back through this list that follows:

Go back to your six streams. This is really important, so spend some time on this section working on each of the streams. This will be your distraction; this will help you create that different map.

How can you remap parts of your day? How can you change the emotion in certain parts of your day? – if you are triggered by a sadness later in the day, create a situation each day that will lift you. If you tend to drink after a stressful day, create another way of destressing, actually talk to yourself during the day so you aren't feeding yourself the same story. Tell yourself you are going to do something different today.

It won't be as simple as just planning the activity, you have to get your mind onboard with it. And to do that you have to talk to your chimp to get him to agree.

Action steps and journal prompts

- What is on your mind? Talk logically to those thoughts. They are just thoughts. Write them down.

- Really ask yourself what you can put into your life to replace the void. If you are struggling, it is very likely there is some sort of void, and it has to be filled.

- You cannot control what happens around you, but you can control how you react to it. Write down those triggering reactions and see if you can extract the chimp from that scenario and replace it with the human.

If the answer is no, you don't think you are ready for change yet, then you have a few options. You could read the book again, possibly giving it more headspace and more time to do the exercises. It also might help to look into certain therapies that might support you in this experience. You might be self-sabotaging, and we need to get you beyond that point. Connecting with one of the sober groups online, tuning in to some of the sober podcasts - this might also help as you start realising you are not alone in this.

Part V

Tools

Part III looked at how the brain and mind responds to alcohol consumption. Part IV looked at creating that positive viewpoint, that positive future image for our minds to latch onto. Now we engage in some tools to support the continued experience.

Lesson 5

Recognising and overcoming triggers and cravings

Whilst most of us have some understanding of triggers and cravings, the science behind them is a little complicated. It is however one of the biggest fears we have around giving up alcohol: that we will be triggered and slip up. So, I would like you to really understand what they are, and how you can recognise your own triggers and cravings and start to reduce/eliminate them.

Identify and understand

First of all, what are they? How and why do they happen? Once we understand the science, we can expose alcohol for what it is – an inconvenient saboteur.

A trigger is a stimulus derived from a thought or a memory.
An alcohol craving is a mental or physical desire to consume alcohol.
A habit then forms as the triggers act like cues, and you find yourself drinking regularly.

So, these triggers can really get in your way when you are trying to change a habit. But if you learn from them or even pre-empt them and adjust the plan accordingly, then the trigger is disarmed.

When you act on a trigger your motivation to follow through on a craving outweighs your reason not to. Sometimes even the most powerful reasons not to drink can be sabotaged by a trigger. Your urge is overcome by a lack of control in that moment.

Alcohol craving is complicated. It comes in layers:

The physical cravings: this is the craving that the **body** has when it feels withdrawal symptoms. As we discussed in Lesson 1, with regular drinking the body has physically adapted to rely on alcohol. It becomes dependent on it so when you stop you feel withdrawal and crave alcohol to fix this. There is a link between that hangover feeling and the physical craving because with a regular drinking habit part of the hangover experience is considered to be withdrawal: your body signalling that you need a top up. The physical cravings can be intense for a few days when the body has none of the alcohol that it has been relying on in its system. They do however pass after one and two weeks depending on your previous consumption.

Psychological cravings: these are tied to the **mental** and **emotional** aspects of drinking and can last much longer. I tell you this because I want you to understand this is why it's so important to follow through on the action steps I list after each lesson. You have literally trained your mind to respond by wanting a drink in so many situations and now we need to retrain it.

The next step is to acknowledge the triggers that might awaken the cravings.

The previous two lessons looked at rewriting the map and changing the picture so there we are beginning to weaken the triggers. That is a really important step for this lesson.

So, it is worth planning ahead to situations that you know will trigger you. It's worth identifying those triggers now, rather than waiting for them to disarm you in the moment.

External triggers: these would be advertising, social situations, places that you specifically associate with alcohol. They might even be smells, songs, films. I can name many films that used to trigger me, because they would take me back to childhood and I would drink to forget those memories. A mild sadness is still triggered when I see certain films. But that sadness trigger used to lead to an alcohol craving. It doesn't anymore. I haven't eliminated feelings associated with memories, but I have eliminated the link to alcohol. This can be a difficult lesson, but if you can identify your own triggers, we can expose them and then engage our human to support us.

Emotional triggers: memories, people, images may trigger an emotional response that you then feel compelled to drink in response to.

Feelings triggered: boredom, tiredness, loneliness to name a few. You will have a memory of responding with alcohol to a number of different feelings. These feelings can weaken us generally when they pop up and our mind may seek to respond as it always has.

The mind is stronger when it knows what will happen (we discussed how our minds avoid the fear of the unknown) so just by opening up to these triggers now, just by thinking about them you are building the strength to tackle any triggers and cravings that might pop up.

So, we have established that so many things trigger us to drink. Drinking is basically an automatic response to these specific stimuli.

With the physical craving your brain has told you that alcohol will fill the gap. When that physical association passes, your mind continues to tell you the same story: that it will relax you, is needed when you are in the pub as much as a vehicle is needed to drive, is needed to heal a hurt the same as medicine would, to make you funnier the same way a personality transplant would, but really it does none of those things, not really. You just do it because you have always done it that is all. It is a habit. Just a habit. Combined with a society that has normalised it and powerful advertising that unhelpfully influences your perception. So, let's address those triggers and cravings.

Action steps and journal prompts

- **Challenge the trigger**: it relaxes me? For how long? Am I bored? What else could relax me? Write a list of possibilities. Try new forms of relaxing. Really take the time to think about what you might find relaxing: reading, yoga, swimming to name a few suggestions.

- **Write down your personal triggers**: after-work drinks, relaxing in front of the TV, going on a date, after a difficult conversation with a family member.

- **Come back into the present**: If you are being taken back to memories and know you are going to be triggered, come back into this moment. Ground yourself. Think of a grounding technique, whether it is breathing, listening to music, or a podcast. I found noise is an amazing distraction and would listen to audio books when cooking dinner as this time was a big trigger for me.

- **Remember the outcomes:** you know it won't end well. You know this is a momentary weakness. Your mind will try to forget your reasons not to drink, both the negatives around drinking and the positives around what you will gain so you have to recall them.

- **Create a mantra:** what simple phrase could you tell yourself or more specifically your chimp? This is of course personal but try it if it will help – "I deserve more", "I am writing a different map", "alcohol doesn't help me", "stand down chimp!"

- **Pre-empt the trigger:** Look for a cue during the day. If you start to notice your mind thinking about alcohol, catch it in the act and respond to it then and there before it gains power. Then with that information try to break down that cue so that it doesn't happen again.

- **Look at yourself in parts:** see the section on Internal Family Systems - What part of me is feeling this? How can I respond to it without drinking? What does it need?

- **Control the frequency of those triggers by changing things up:** create a life where the triggers don't feel as powerful, where they don't feel welcome.

> • But whatever you do, **"Don't lean into the craving"**

Removing triggers and cravings has to be done with positivity. Without boring you again, don't forget removing alcohol is all positive. There is absolutely nothing negative about removing it from your life. But I don't want you to feel negative about the position you are in either. Alcohol is a legalised addictive substance that we are encouraged to consume. It is a pesky little molecule (called ethanol) that, because of its size, can have an extremely diverse range of effects on the body and mind and can be very unpredictable. That's why it will have one effect on one person and an entirely different effect on someone else. So, let's lose any negative feelings here. This is not your fault. Your body is responding to a chemical the way it was designed to.

Action steps and journal prompts

1.Positively change the map to reduce your cravings: There will be times of day that you associate with drinking more strongly than others. Certain elements of your day will be **hardwired** to contain an alcoholic drink. It is what you have always done. It is what your brain will look for and your mind will want. It may be that you have had a drink at a particular time of day for decades. It has become a ritual, so embedded in your life that to stop doing it without any thought or plan in place is going to feel strange. You might even feel a sense of loss. So we need to rewrite the map, change those moments in your day.

2.Loss or any negative feeling from removing alcohol is something that we want to challenge. If the feeling comes up, we need to acknowledge it. The Internal Family Systems theory comes up here. Remember that there may be parts of you that haven't come to terms with letting go of the alcohol. There may be parts of you that are still picturing a "relaxing" you or a "more social" you. That's okay. We will come across how to tackle this in the next lesson on ambivalence. It may feel like there is a downside but if done right there are really only positives. There is nothing negative about removing or reducing alcohol in your life, but you may not have reached the point where you are completely feeling that yet.

3.What do we do with those pinch moments? We need to completely change the routine, change the map, and confuse our brain. Let's look at a simple scenario. If you normally:

- Walk the dog

- Cook dinner

- Then have a glass of wine

Then try changing these steps. Cook dinner and then walk the dog. If you always sit down on the sofa in the evening with a drink to watch TV, I strongly suggest you take a few weeks off that routine. It will be difficult to follow through with that same routine minus the drink. Decide to do something completely different in those early days. Changing the steps changes the path in your mind. Find an alternative activity in the evening if that is your trigger. Immerse yourself in some new learning. Arrange to meet someone for a walk, sign up to a course, plan a decluttering exercise in your home. It doesn't matter what it is just make it different.

4. Exhaust yourself by getting up super early and going to bed early if evenings trigger you. I honestly highly suggest this one. Rewrite the elements of your day for a while, rewrite how you structure it. We are incredibly habitual until we question the habit and suggest something different. I think there is something really powerful about getting up early anyway when you have a clear head and more energy. You could carve out some really special time just for you, and the flipside is that you are tired in the evening and can go to bed early in those early days. I signed up to so many online courses when I stopped drinking. I hadn't done anything like that before, but I really wanted to put the time to good use, to distract my mind and do something completely different so I was changing the map. Whatever it takes. But don't follow the same routine and expect your brain not to reach for the familiar element of a glass of wine. Your brain follows paths, and if you go down the same path it will need a drink.

Do not just do nothing and white knuckle it! As I said, years of pre-conditioning. Years of ritual. It won't work to just hope your mind likes the new you and goes along with it.

- Change around the elements of your evening, as I said before, in terms of when you do things and in which order.

- Increase or start an exercise routine at the triggering time of day. Join a class.

- Try out a totally new hobby.

- Replace the routine drink with alcohol-free alternatives.

This might feel simplistic, so build a story around these bullet points. Make life interesting. Engage your brain in something else. Maybe this feels like a lot of effort, but the reward is that you are engaging in something new, distracting your mind, confusing your brain. Trying new things also has the added benefit of firing up your inspiration. It makes us feel good to challenge ourselves, to take ourselves out of our comfort zones so the more creative you can be with this extra time the better.

Engaging in this lesson was life changing for me, empowering and energising. I joined a public speaking group and faced a fear there. I joined a local running club to push my running comfort zone (and made some fabulous connections in the process). I started having a weekly friend catch-up at 5.30am online as we had both become early risers. In the early days I would walk the dog early as I came to really love the peace of the early morning. I signed up for a course on Buddhism, Stoicism, and a bunch more, and the more I did, the more excited I became about what I could achieve. So, challenging these trigger moments has a second massive upside (the first of course being not drinking).

5. Stop! What is the trigger really telling you? You have your alcohol-free drinks, your quit lit, you are drowning out your chattering chimp with podcasts. You have re-mapped some of those triggering habitual parts of your day to banish the alcohol. Now I want you to question what the trigger is really telling you. A trigger might be associated with a need, so we want to make sure we understand that need and are fulfilling it in other ways to avoid us feeling lacking in some way further down the line. Let's think of some scenarios:

If you come home from work and you "need a drink". Do you need to decompress from a crazy workday? Have you had a particularly stressful day? Would going for a walk improve that? What would a chat with a friend do? Could you sit in stillness and breathe? Can you still sit down, relax and watch a program with an alcohol free drink? I used to love doing a free online yoga program in the evenings now and again. Or a hot bath. There are so many ways to relax, we just forgot about them when we replaced them with alcohol.

Of course, pouring an alcoholic drink feels like the natural way to go because, again, this is what society tells us to do and what we have always done. If the drink gave us the relaxation without any of the other side effects, then maybe that would be a solution. But if you are seeking instant relaxation, you would only need a small amount of alcohol. Alcohol goes straight to your bloodstream and instantly travels around your body. It won't take long for that feeling to kick in. But you know you don't just have just one and that is the problem.

So, pouring a drink is not the solution to that post-work need to relax so you need to find another solution.

Are you nervous about an event and want to drink to cope? Are you actually overthinking the event? What are you nervous about? Can you identify key elements? Try not to have just a general worry, but to identify whether it's the volume of people or the specific group of people, getting there and parking or what to wear. Can you alleviate any of the stress points? Could you shorten the time you are there or possibly decline the invitation if you are in the early days?

Have you had some bad news and need a drink to cope? I discussed this in Lesson 1 but whilst alcohol initially suppresses neurotransmitters in the brain to essentially numb your feelings and thoughts, long term it also suppresses the feel-good hormones so it ends up making you feel worse, much worse. A better solution in the early days would be a distraction to take your mind away from a situation if that is needed at the time. Distract rather than numb. Long term we learn to experience all the feelings in the sober world and that can feel uncomfortable at first, but the overriding impression is that it is easier to cope with situations sober.

Are you just bored? Habit literally fills the boredom gap. Just give it a little thought and do something else to fill the gap.

Whatever your feelings are, you are going to have to practise thinking a lot more before you act on them. This can really prove a useful tool with the rest of your life, and I hope you start to notice that. Becoming more aware and more considered in your actions can be so much more energising than living in a fog on automatic pilot.

6. Positive planning. Don't dread occasions. Look forward to the plan. Consider how you might handle different scenarios that will crop up. As I said before there will **ALWAYS** be a reason to drink, so plan ahead as to how you will handle those different situations.

7. Distraction tactics. Despite all best intentions, trigger moments can come from nowhere. The chimp can pop up unexpectedly. The firefighters can step in to try to support you by suggesting a drink. They think they are helping. It's what you have always done.

So, we need to support those parts that are still struggling at times, and the best way I have found is honest distraction. Call it a toolbox, call it a rescue mission - whatever you want to call it, the aim is to distract you from those triggering thoughts, when your chimp mind invites you for, or even insists you have a drink.

So, what does this distraction strategy look like? Well whatever works for you. What plans can you put in place that you can go to in the spur of the moment? I mentioned before it is always worth having options should you need them. We are all different so your toolbox might be very different to mine, but I will share some of the tools I used:

- Courses on online learning platforms -There are so many

courses in every subject you can imagine. I did a lot of courses when I stopped drinking. It reassured me that instead of drinking I was learning something new with my time.

- Running (replace with any exercise)- Pushing yourself on the exercise front can really help your mindset as you see you are able to achieve so much more physically.

- Coffees, dinners, dog walks - I think I ended up seeing my friends more when I realised I wasn't confined to drinking nights out.

- House project - mine was decluttering - I watched the two "Minimalist" documentaries on Netflix and away I went. It completely changed the way I view my possessions and was a brilliant mind clearing distraction.

So, let's notice those triggers and learn from them so we eventually disarm them.

Lesson 6

Overcoming ambivalence

> Ambivalence: "The state of having two opposing feelings at the same time, or being uncertain about how you feel"

Why do people find it so hard to moderate their alcohol intake or to give up entirely? The answer is often ambivalence. It keeps you caught in an equilibrium of opposing forces. On the one hand you might know not drinking is a good idea. On the other hand, society, friends, your own chimp is telling you not to stop. Both sides might have strong influences. So where does that leave you? Firmly in the middle!

Ambivalence is considered a part of the process with behavioural change, so it is not unexpected that it crops up during the Sober Experience. Change can be understood as a cost benefit equation, and until we have re-framed the costs or have eliminated them, we are stuck with the see-saw of equilibrium. If there didn't exist two sides to this giving up, then it wouldn't be hard.

So, we know we are considering a change, or we wouldn't be here. We have talked so far in the book about the brain, the mind, the triggers and cravings and the emergence of the open mindset, the chimp, and those firefighters. We have talked about changing the map to direct ourselves away from those cravings and to appease the chimp. But that work is of no use if ambivalence kicks in. So, let's look at what we perceive are those **opposing feelings** around alcohol, or more simply our perceived benefits and disadvantages of not drinking.

In the sober coaching world, we like to use the visual aid of a see-saw where we highlight the benefits you perceive of giving up on one side and the disadvantages on the other. So, let's get started.

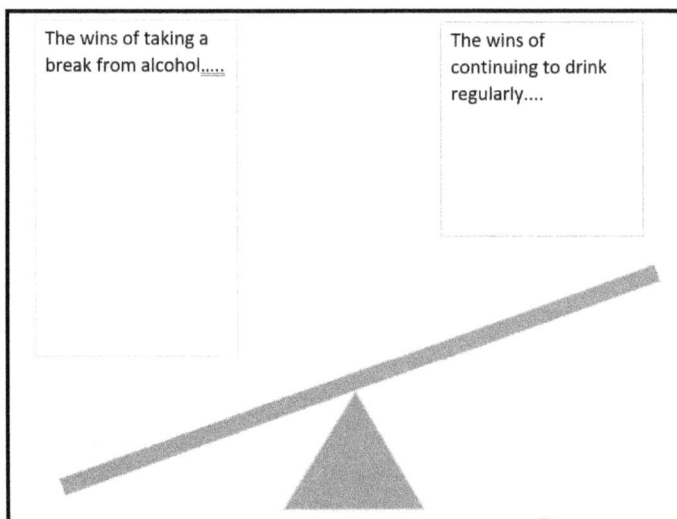

The wins of taking a break from alcohol.....

The wins of continuing to drink regularly....

Action steps and journal prompts

1)Drawing the see-saw
Draw your own ambivalence see-saw in your notebook
On the left side of the see-saw write down all of the positives you can think of around giving up or cutting back on alcohol

On the right side write down all of the perceived disadvantages of giving up

2) The left side of the see-saw

The positives. Really think hard here, dig deep. The more convincing your argument to not drink, the easier it will be to stop. Widen the lens beyond the obvious lack of hangover, money saving or whatever springs instantly to mind. Here are a few pointers to widen that lens:

Sleep - have you noticed it yet? Yes, not drinking has a huge impact on your sleep - both the quality and the length of sleep. And sleep opens up your mornings and gives you so much more time.

Positivity - your mindset is massively impacted by drinking less. Life is physically and mentally less of a strain, so those positives are easier to find.

Connection - the clarity that comes with not drinking makes every connection you make so much stronger if you choose it to be. You listen more, you have more patience. You may even feel like you care more as you are making more room for other people's emotions when you lift the fog.

Nutrition - how does a reduction in alcohol positively impact your nutrition? Does it make you think more consciously about what else you put into your body? Are you less inclined to reach for comfort snacks when you aren't drinking as much? As I write this, this is one I have yet to crack so I am not saying all of these changes are guaranteed!

Movement - drinking less 100% leads to more energy which in turn should lead to more movement generally. But what have you specifically noticed? Do you move between tasks more easily? Do you jump out of bed with more energy? Do you feel you can take on more exercise?

Recovery - this is the time that you give to yourself to decompress, to unwind. You are more likely to be kinder to yourself when you cut back on drinking so this might naturally flow through to allow yourself time and space to recover. You might start to think more about what you need. When you stop going through your normal routines and start to question your actions there is a high chance you will want to start prioritising yourself more and what you need in your day to reset and recover. This is a really important step for your mind set during the Sober Experience. Recovery gives you mental strength which supports the experience.

So the idea is that we make the see-saw weigh down in favour of the positives i.e. more positives of giving up to negatives of giving up. But we will include a few for completeness...

3) The right side of the see-saw

To avoid us sitting on the ambivalence fence, we really need to look at cracking those right-side reasons and breaking them down. What have you written down? Take each reason in turn and really think about it. Would removing alcohol really cause a negative impact in this way? Could you in fact turn it around to a positive? Some examples from previous groups where I have carried out this exercise are:

Alcohol gives me confidence - this is a myth. The confidence gained from going against societal expectations and tackling your alcohol use should be worth so much more than the confidence alcohol gives you. The confidence from being clear headed and energised is huge.

Alcohol makes the event more fun - but you are still with your friends, you are still experiencing the same event. All you are not doing is dulling your senses which effectively is what alcohol does. It depresses your senses and takes the edge off everything. Do you really need that to enjoy the evening? It might feel strange at first, but you will be fine without it.

Alcohol calms me down - yes it depresses certain neurotransmitters in your brain called GABA - in the very short term you may feel calmer, but this happens instantly with an extremely low volume. As your consumption increases, the impact to your brain changes as your body can't process the alcohol quickly enough.

4) Banish the ambivalence

I want you to drill down on those reasons that lead you to drink. Question every single one of them. Take time over this exercise. Alcohol can be quite compelling, but only on the face of it. When you really start to interrogate those benefits the argument falls apart.

If you have completed the see-saw exercise I hope you have squashed some of those reasons on the right side - those reasons why you would want to carry on drinking. It is really important that you do this exercise. If you don't, we come back to sitting in the middle of the fence and being **ambivalent.** The chimp will use any ambivalence to weaken you when tempted. Ambivalence gives us the excuse, lets us off the goal that we are going for.

Lesson 7

It's not a slip up, it's a learning experience

This lesson involves recognising that the road might not be a straight one, so what do we do with the information gained from any blips along the way?

It isn't day 1, it's the continued experience

I have already mentioned that I don't use terms like "back to square 1", "day 1", "here we go again". You are not at the beginning. How could you possibly be unless you really are experiencing this for the first time. But otherwise, you are here where you are right now. What have you learnt? What might you do differently? What things might you add to the experience to support a more positive direction? What learning can you use so that you can adapt the process? So often the drivers to drink are in our subconscious. They are hidden away. By bringing them to the surface we are letting them know that we want to expose them. This can be difficult at times, and yet again I caveat that if recognising your triggers does throw up some difficult memories, some form of therapy would be advised. But we have to look at what caused the blip if we want to avoid it again. By at least recognising that an experience, a pattern of behaviour or a memory might be triggering you to drink, we can choose to say that we don't want that anymore. We can then take the step to replace it, or we can seek support, but ignoring it will prevent us from progressing.

Fear of the unknown

I mentioned this as a potential barrier in Lesson 3. Our minds like to know what is going to happen. If you have relied on alcohol for a long period of time, removing it is unknown territory, and our minds fear that. We go into fight or flight mode. The feeling is unfamiliar. Even though we know we want to stop, that fear can be powerful. You might not be aware that fear is pulling you back, but if you pause to think about it, could that possibly be the problem? The fight would be to face that fear which is what I am going to suggest. The flight would of course be to give in to the urge and have a drink, and we do this because the fear feels overwhelming. So, in the action step we look at what we are fearing, what exactly could go wrong if we give it a try and we sit with those feelings so the fear lessens.

Fabricating a story that leads to drink

It isn't that you deserve a drink because of what has happened to you, it is often that you have created a story, a pathway if you like, that leads to drink. You have told yourself that alcohol is a fix.

What I hadn't realised was that the stories I had told myself to justify my drinking habit had a profound impact on my daily actions, on my memories and on the vision of my future. Let me explain; I was rewarding myself for a difficult day with my children, so my days really felt more difficult. Or at least the story I would tell myself as I poured that glass of wine was "You deserve this," and so the memory of my days became difficult. I will repeat this. The brain wants the easiest path to a drug so it will smooth the way at every opportunity. Embellishing the memory of a day will do just that.

So then of course you expect the next day to be the same. I would go as far as to say that your subconscious hopes the next day will be the same, and one step further you make it the same. I have seen on many occasions people playing out that path leading to alcohol.

Action steps and journal prompts

Questions: What are you telling yourself is your reason for drinking? What are you telling yourself is the reason it is so hard to stop? Can you engage your human here and rationalise this feeling? Alcohol will not help the situation.

Fear ladder: What are the things you are most afraid of around drinking? Rank them in order from most frightening to least. You can start by working on the thing that frightens you the least. Work through them in your notebook, visualise them and take the energy out of them. Slowly work through the fears lessening their power.

The temporary point of no return

Once our minds are set, we have moved into chimp mode and it is very difficult to put the brakes on in that moment. Alcohol is addictive and that chimp is powerful. He has eradicated all the negatives attached to alcohol. He has told you you very much deserve it. It is extremely difficult to stop when you get to THAT stage. So where is that stage for you? What are the signs that lead up to it? What is that initial story you are telling yourself before the momentum builds? How can we put the brakes on at that point? I see it often. The powerful reason that you should have a drink, that you need to have a drink will have been building. It is unlikely that it just happens, so it is important to put the brakes on before it gathers momentum. Tune in to when that mindset is starting to shift not when it has completely turned.

Act on the information

If you want this and you can learn to tune into YOUR mind, you will crack this. But it's about being honest with your thoughts, understanding your triggers and then most importantly, responding to this information. Think about it. In any aspect of life, if you know something is not working you do it differently. This is no different.

I am not living in a petri dish

Give yourself a break. I have given you all the logic, the compelling reasons to stop and you can't! Why ever not? Well, isn't it obvious? You aren't in a chemistry lab sitting in isolation. It isn't just me that is feeding you information. Your senses are being stimulated all the time, the awareness of alcohol around you heightened even by reading this book, but I hope the awareness from my side will quickly turn into a compelling support against drinking. Some days the temptation might feel greater than it did before you embarked on this experience because you might feel like it is in your thoughts constantly. But the switch will flick if you keep working on it. Eventually you will continue to think about alcohol, but in recognising how incredible life is without it. But in the short term it might take a little time to work through the thought hijacking.

Act on the blip

If you have had a drink recently, right now alcohol might be in your system. You are thinking with a hangover. This is not a helpful, strong position to make any decisions from. But when you feel ready, consider repeating the lessons, altering parts of your day to start re-writing the map, considering again all that you have to gain from this experience.

What not to do

- Do not hide away.

- Do not feel shame. Alcohol is addictive pure and simple. There is no shame in being drawn to a socially acceptable drug.

- Do not give up. I have said so many times this doesn't have to be an instant success. There is learning in the experience however long it takes.

- Do not feel alone. There is a whole world of sober adventurers out there.

CHECKPOINT

We talked about autopilot at the beginning of the book. It's a mind and brain state that you are all too familiar with. So even as you are working through this book be careful not to slip into autopilot. I don't mean that you should be on alcohol alert the whole time, I just mean please keep pushing yourself to take those positive steps, to create those action points to level up your daily life, and to implement changes that really will create a different life. So now and again I want you to check in.

Let's take the learning so far and see where it puts you: How strong are you feeling?

Triggers and cravings: Have you put those plans in place to address these? Do you need to do more work on that?

Where do you want to be?: Can you picture an energy level you want to reach, a tangible thing you want to achieve? - anything that puts you into the future looking at a life that can only be achieved without alcohol.

Morning routines: I appreciate we are not all morning people, however I would suggest adopting this concept for a while as, whether you are a morning person or not, everyone's morning is enhanced by the absence of a hangover. Also, getting up earlier makes you more tired in the evening, so if evening is your trigger time you can adjust your bedtime in the short term.

The six streams: Remember my concept of sitting in a dark room and trying to remove alcohol. By looking at the six streams you are keeping yourself balanced from a wellbeing perspective. This will allow you to put those new energies to the best use. So check in and score yourself on those before we move on.

It is really important that you check in honestly here with how you are feeling before we move on.

Part VI
Continuing the adventure

The next section is really about taking life up a gear if you are feeling stronger now. I am not suggesting you have read Parts I to V and feel ready to receive the new you without hesitation. But.... if you have read the first five Parts then I hope you have resonated with some of the words, have taken on board the learnings and are starting to feel stronger. Combined with you having a period without alcohol in your system, you are likely to be feeling physically and mentally stronger. So, I would love you to start using some of that energy to begin creating that positive future vision - start exploring the new destination. Because if we don't push forward with this next lesson, the temptation will be to slip up as there is nothing enticing pulling you forward, nothing inviting you to carry on.

If you don't feel you are ready yet, then please take the time to re-read Parts I to V.

Lesson 8

The Four Energies

Increased energy is one of the biggest wins when you kick alcohol out the door, but what exactly does energy look like in this new life?

I don't think I really appreciated how much alcohol impacted my energy levels until I considered what energy actually means. I said before that I likened having a regular drinking habit to being in the back seat of my life, and that is because I simply wasn't fully engaged in my life. Alcohol had taken up the driving seat and I let myself be controlled by it.

So, when you remove that level of control, when you put yourself back in the driving seat the effect is monumental. It's important that you take the time to acknowledge it, otherwise, it can quickly become the new normal. We are so quick to highlight the lows but dampen down the wins. But the power and the longevity of this change is in acknowledging how big it is and how much of a positive impact it has had on your life. It all comes down to energy gains.

Dr Jim Loehr (1) identified four separate but interconnected sources of energy, and when I considered this and how they are impacted by alcohol it was yet another lightbulb moment.

Physical energy – the physical power you feel in your movement, your strength, your endurance, your stamina. Regularly consuming alcohol drains you physically - from the impact on sleep, to the pain in your liver, to the sickness from hangover and your weakened immune system. Your movement is slower when you drink, you move with less conviction, less certainty, less confidence. You will be feeling so much more physically strong now.

Emotional energy – how balanced you feel. The way you handle everyday situations and are able to cope with life, the big stuff, and the small irritations, is likely to be so different now. I believe removing alcohol raises your baseline, which is the level that you fall to when things get tough, and so you bounce back so much quicker. You don't have the chemical messengers tampering with your brain and affecting your emotions. You don't have the mental pull and constant battle between your human and your chimp.

Mental energy – how focused you feel. Hangovers massively affect how we focus, our co-ordination and our ability to respond. So, your mental energy is hugely depleted when you have been drinking heavily. The mental ability to cope with problems at home, work, and to listen and respond.

Spiritual energy – the force of your energy gained from following your values, your beliefs. Are you able to channel your focus where you want it to go rather than be carried along with the general flow? Lifting the fog of alcohol can reveal some real clarity in this area, an area which you had perhaps never considered before.

When you remove alcohol there is a positive impact on all of these energy flows. Where we might struggle with ambivalence is often when we don't really consider all of these energies individually, where we haven't fully acknowledged the power of removing alcohol. Ambivalence comes from ignoring all of the benefits so to avoid continuing the experience. We are going to focus on those energies now so that it gives us the drive to continue as we recognise how much more energised we really do feel.

Action steps and journal prompts

Think about those four energies

Consider how reducing alcohol has impacted each of them. Take time to consider and reflect.

With the physical energy, do you find your days are longer so you can achieve so much more, able to incorporate more movement into your day, or simply the speed and strength with which you move through the day?

With emotional energy, we talked about raising your bar before, that invisible floor that you fall to when you are challenged. Do you feel stronger emotionally? Do you recover more quickly?

Mental energy: do you feel that you are able to bring out your human more regularly? To feel more balanced, more able to focus? More logical in thought and response.

Spiritual energy: do you feel you have the strength to live by the things you value more? Saying no to the pull of alcohol really helps to make life a little clearer. It might then begin to clarify your thoughts around what you value.

Again, we are all different and we are all reading this book from a different current perspective, so I put this lesson out there for consideration. There will come a point, if you do benefit from a decent period without alcohol, that you will have a boost in these four energies, and I want you to really notice that. Alcohol may have removed the blinkers but as already discussed, we do as humans have that tendency to not notice some pretty fundamental positive changes that happen to us. We are not very good at stopping and celebrating the success.

What to do with that energy

Of course we need to direct this new energy somewhere. We need a new focus for our focus! When alcohol lifts the veil, you become so much more aware. Combine that with the energy and all the extra time you have gained, and you have a powerful new resource that needs a clear direction. So, think about where you want to direct this energy. Give it careful consideration. Think of it as a new superpower, a gift.

Early mornings

By this point I am really hoping you have noticed glorious sleep being one of the by-products of reducing your alcohol intake. It really is incredible the impact removing that one thing can have, and not just on the specific act of sleeping, but the mindset in which you go to bed, the mood, the positivity. It all equates to going off to sleep with a more rested mind. For me I often don't sleep fully through the night, but I find that I am able to function so much better on less sleep! So, it can go either way.

Part of changing my map was to start getting up early to make the most of my mornings before the rest of the house woke up. I took it to the extreme (by my standards) at the start of my Sober Experience and then reined myself in. It started with me leaping out of my comfort zone and following Hal Elrod's miracle morning (2). Elrod prescribes getting up early (I picked 5am) to do a series of exercises involving a bit of journaling, actual exercise, and a few other elements. I did it for a whole year to help kick start my new map. Whilst I didn't stick to it exactly, what it did do is change my whole concept of time. I realised this was to do with the pressure that was released when I stopped drinking. Drinking creates so much diary management: Do I have a busy workday the next day? Do I need to get up early for an appointment? Do I need to pick any of my children up late at night etc., etc. Change your relationship with alcohol and you have a totally blank canvas. You have time and energy. You can carve out a piece of time for **you** every day. I realised I could actually get up early any morning of the week. I realised I had so much more flexibility to manage the different elements of my life. So for that first year I got up at 5am, and followed a morning routine. It would have sounded insane to the person I was a year prior, but at that time in my life it was a positive challenge I wanted to try. I have dipped in and out of early mornings over the years since I stopped drinking. My family dynamic will shift, life gets busier and I might feel I need more sleep, but I always try to come back to my early mornings as I have found them so beneficial to me. When you stop drinking you feel the flexibility of constantly being able to adapt and make positive changes. I feel real freedom in knowing I have the energy to create a new structure whenever I like.

Creating a morning routine really set me up for the day, there is no doubt about it. As with the wake-up times, it creates an anchor point for you. Whatever else happens in your day, there is a solid piece of the day that no one can influence.

Take more time

So you have more energy which means you have more time, can you finally take the time to figure out what you might want to do with it? Exercise, learning, socialising, reading, volunteering, gardening, painting.

Think about what you might have enjoyed in a prior life, think about what is on your to do list but you have never actually done it.

Lesson 9

Enjoying the freedom of control

"This sounds crazy! Alcohol is addictive. There is nothing to do with control here apart from that it has control over me!"

But let me give you a different perspective, a perspective which I really hope will make you change the dialogue in your mind.

As I was in the midst of writing this book, a realisation came to me. This Sober Experience was the first thing I had control over. I was in the position I was in because of all the things I didn't have control over but this thing – that I initially thought was a battle and came to realise was the biggest blessing to ever happen to my life – this was all mine.

So how does alcohol take that control?

You may have been:-

- Drinking to cope - you had created a dialogue in your head that told you alcohol will help

- Drinking because of your past - out of habit or to numb a pain

- Because there is nothing else - again I suggest this is due to the blinkering effect

But why is alcohol behind these stories?

As we discussed in lesson 1:

1. It is the withdrawal effect of alcohol that makes you unable to cope without it in your system once it has become a habit.

2. It is the depressant effect that depresses your emotions making it feel like a good fit for someone that wants to drown out the noise of unpleasant memories. What we don't realise is that alcohol goes on to create hangxiety, withdrawal and make those low feelings worse.

3. I liken drinking alcohol to wearing blinkers. How can you have full control of your thoughts and reactions when you are only really **seeing** a fraction of life. You can't be in control when you aren't fully aware.

Alcohol gains control over lives in every way. Remove it and you regain control over your life. I would like you to stop and acknowledge this. It can feel empowering, overwhelming and for me, completely mind blowing. It turns out it wasn't just a drink when I felt like it, it was a controlling habit that impacted life around the habit in so many ways.

But you must remember...

Removing the alcohol can't change everything

It's important to know this and to acknowledge it. I have already mentioned that alcohol has a clever way of latching on to a problem and telling you that you deserve a drink. A common journey for some might be that they feel like they are flying through their Sober Experience, until a problem arises in their life and the faithful response returns - a drink. Firstly, we have now learnt why this has happened in the lessons around fear and our mind's response to seek comfort in the well-trodden path.

You might be struggling in your life right now with some problems which are really significant for you. They might be really big for anyone. Removing the alcohol won't take those problems away, but it will impact you in some very powerful ways and I want you to acknowledge these so that you change the story in your mind and feel that control.

"Removing alcohol cannot change everything but it will make me stronger"

Removing alcohol has the effect of ...

Raising your bar. "Well, you recovered a lot quicker from that one" said my husband after another interaction with my mum. I used to find my relationship with my mum completely debilitating. I would be left exhausted, powerless, and incredibly sad after an encounter with her. Now I still feel sad, but it doesn't paralyse me. Removing the alcohol empowers you to cope better. Removing alcohol lightens the weight of the ....

The stone in my pocket: Jay Shetty (Coach, Podcaster, former Monk) mentioned this on a podcast. He talked of a friend who describes grief as a stone in your pocket. It's always there, but as you get stronger the stone feels lighter. I think this analogy can be applied to many struggles. I think removing the alcohol has made the stone lighter, and I controlled that. Because I know where alcohol is concerned ......

It just won't enhance the situation in ANY way: You won't sleep well. Your physical energy will be impacted. You will experience 'hangxiety' the next day. It will awaken your chimp making you react impulsively and become easily provoked. There is no control there. Remove the alcohol and you remove ....

The ripple effect: So consider adding alcohol to a situation as creating a ripple effect. If the situation is already a struggle, why pick up an enormous weight and make it harder for yourself. The heavier the weight the bigger the ripples will be when you throw it in the water. When times are tough don't you deserve a little self-care? Having a drink isn't self-care. Don't you deserve to have....

Control over your reactions? Having a drink makes you lose control of your emotions and reactions. Your brain is being hijacked, being flooded with additional Dopamine and GABA as we discussed in the Brain lesson. This has a huge negative effect on emotions. Removing the alcohol means you can actually control your emotions.

So this is what I mean by control, and it's important to acknowledge its significance. So often we drink out of despair, out of a feeling that we don't have control with situations in our lives and we don't like that feeling. So we drink to drown it out. In that instant, in that tiny moment, that action will do the trick. But it is a momentary solution, nothing more. Removing the alcohol will make you realise there are some things you can control - how you respond, how you gain strength, where you shine your light. But adding alcohol to a difficult situation is not a solution.

Action steps and journal prompts

How do you feel removing alcohol has brought some control back into your life?

Do you feel you are more in control of your emotions, your responses, your time, your decisions?

We can actually control very little in life, but we control how we respond to life and when alcohol intervenes it sabotages that process. It takes away the control over your responses. By removing alcohol, you are giving yourself that control back.

Lesson 10

Climb your own mountain

What does the mountain look like to you?

It is a common theme in the alcohol-free world to climb a mountain and the symbolism shouldn't be lost. Achievement, success, accomplishment. The size, the height, the impact. Yes, a mountain will do it, but it can also be a metaphor. So many sober acquaintances have gone on to run marathons, move to new countries, walk hundreds of kilometres, change careers. The door opens, the fog clears, the veil is lifted. I myself run a lot more. That is my outlet. It rebalances me. But those same people including me would talk for hours about the little changes – the relationships, the daily improvements, the energy, noticing the sunrises. The big-ticket items – well they simply started as a distraction that grew and grew, the icing on the cake or the snow on the mountain. Your mountain might be a feeling, a new hobby you have always dreamed of taking up, new positive routines with your children, new connections, volunteering with all the extra time you have. There is a mountain for absolutely everyone.

My mountain

Well actually there was a real-life mountain – two in fact – Snowden and Scafell Pike in the UK, and they were fun to climb. But on those two trips, the actual bonus wasn't the mountain. It was the people I climbed with - a bunch of new friends that I had made in the alcohol-free space. I wasn't actually in the market for making new friends, but something about the authenticity of being sober, the common thread that connects sober people, friendships were made and are now cherished.

But my metaphorical mountain has been climbed in stages. I want to keep making the point that whilst at first glance you may have thought changing your relationship with alcohol is "giving something up", what I hope you have discovered is that it is anything but that. There is nothing to give up and everything to gain.

Because this is a positive experience in every sense of the word: embracing change, stepping into the unknown, facing and dealing with challenges and potential setbacks, noticing achievements along the way. These are all stages of the mountain, of the adventure, of the Sober Experience.

It might not be obviously shiny and bright – one tangible change as such, but I hope you come to realise what you gain is a ripple of so many things and this is what creates the shine. It might take time but every step is learning and that is why I say the most important thing is to notice every positive change that happens along the way.

So you have proved you are up for the Sober Experience by still being here. Let's take it further. Let's get further out of your comfort zone!

Comfort zones

When you are in the comfort zone you are at risk of switching to automatic pilot: you don't have to think, you go with the flow, you do what society tells you to do, and at one point that was a very loud voice permitting you to drink.

Well the "norm" doesn't suit us as we are trying to change the map to remove any potential triggers, so in the comfort zone is not where we want to stay.

So how can you get out of your comfort zone? What new challenges can you take up? If you can train yourself to feel comfortable getting out of your comfort zone you will be more able to embrace the alcohol-free life.

Make it exciting, make it challenging. You have this new energy, clarity, and time. What are you going to do with it?

Adopting that Growth mindset

We already agreed we just cannot stay on the same path, as the chimp will be familiar with this path and the associated alcohol use. We are already embracing this growth mindset.

As I mentioned at the start of the book the growth mindset describes a way of viewing challenges and setbacks. People who have a growth mindset believe that even if they struggle with certain skills, their abilities aren't set in stone. They know they can develop and change.

Adventure, growth, pushing the boundaries has huge benefits:

- It makes you stronger, as you overcome the fears and the uncertainties and realise pushing yourself isn't as scary as you thought it would be.

- It gives you confidence.

- Planning adventures gives you a focus in the future - something to aim for.

So what would you like to plan? Take the time to do some research. Listen to some sober podcasts and hear what others have been up to. Join a club to give you the accountability to achieve that goal.

I encourage you to play along with this step as it gives you that future anchor point. Again there is my version of a monthly goal planner on my website which might motivate you.

So welcome to a different view of life!

To those whose drinking stemmed from past suffering, maybe you have combined a form of therapy with reading this book. I hope when you remove alcohol you will see that whilst you can't change the past, the strength and resilience you will gain from removing alcohol, the change in perspective you will gain from removing the blinkers - these will carry you forward with a new perspective and a different energy that you bring to it all.

To those who have simply got into the habit of drinking regularly. You don't know why, you are not sure how. Maybe there was a life shift that you didn't notice. You might now realise there is no reason other than it's addictive! I hope you will now find life is pretty special without it.

To the parents who thought alcohol was their fuel, I hope you now feel rocket fuelled by not drinking.

To those that found evenings lonely and were filling a void, I hope you find that your time can be utilised in so many other ways and that not drinking brings out that adventurer in you.

To those who are pushing their careers and used alcohol to relax, I hope you have realised that alcohol really gives you the briefest fix and is countered by a whole heap of non-relaxing problems. Taking the time to see what other ways you can relax is far more energising and productive.

If you have read this book, if you have followed the exercises and worked on the chimp, if you have acknowledged the parts of you that struggle and talked to them, if you have strengthened your image of the Sober Experience and embraced it, then you have achieved what this book hoped you would have achieved. That's not to say you might need to read it again, to try to take a complete break if you were just curious. The choice is yours.

CHECKPOINT

Let's diagnose you at this stage

I said before I don't like labels, so what do I mean here? Well imagine you went to the doctor and instead of asking how much alcohol you are consuming they ask about your mindset, whether you can picture life ahead with positivity. We have discussed all of these things already, so this is just a check in and a chance to refresh a lesson if you need to. It's at this point I would ask you if there are any areas where you are struggling, so you know what you still need to focus on.

Struggling to find positive reasons not to drink; focus on Lessons 3 and 4 and the Six Streams. Engage in alcohol free podcasts, join some sober groups online. Tap into the positive energy.

Feelings of anger bubbling up about the position you are in. Read my story, Part I and Lesson 1. I want you to solidify the knowledge that it is addictive, pure and simple.

Focusing on the past. There may be a need for additional therapy. Also go back to Lesson 3.

Drinking significant volumes. Visit your GP to discuss your options. It might be that additional or alternative support might be needed as you reduce your intake.

Struggling to think of how on earth to bring new adventure into your life. See Lesson 9 on Energies. It doesn't have to be big. Small changes can be really powerful. I am not asking you to create a map to journey to the centre of the earth, just to create enough change to lift you, to entice you to do life differently.

Refresh on the Ten Lessons

I created these Ten Lessons to inform you, to send you a message of positivity, to encourage you to acknowledge the changes and to inspire further change. Studying them will help you alter habitual thought patterns that have you hooked into alcohol consumption, gain more energy and optimism and discover the real you.

You can return to the lessons as often as you need - you can study whichever ones feel right for you at the time and move towards a different relationship with alcohol at the pace and in the way that is right for you. So let's refresh those lessons.

Lesson 1: Understanding the link between alcohol and your brain - The effect alcohol has on your brain is powerful and complicated. As you understand this you'll realise any problems you have with alcohol aren't a personal weakness. Knowledge can give you the strength you need to resist cravings and embrace the Sober Experience.

Lesson 2: How to change your mindset around alcohol - We're all made up of different parts. Inside us all we have a Chimp, who is impulsive and reckless, and a Human, who deep down knows that life would be better without alcohol. Learning to recognise and manage these conflicts will help you change your relationship with alcohol for the better.

Lesson 3: Building a story around the statement - You're interested in exploring your relationship with alcohol. But it's important to ask yourself, what's the story behind that? Knowing why you want to change will keep you on track when change feels daunting and your motivation fades.

Lesson 4: Creating a positive picture of a life without alcohol- Rather than focusing on the problems that alcohol can cause, focus on "How would you like your life to change?" Would you like to have more energy and clarity? Focus on the positives, and the changes that would make the most difference to you personally, and paint a new picture of a life without alcohol.

Lesson 5: Recognising and overcoming triggers and cravings - These are powerful, but momentary. By getting to know yourself and your own patterns, you can discover practical techniques, such as using distractions or planning other activities that will mean it's you, not alcohol that is in control.

Lesson 6: Overcoming ambivalence: Take a deep-dive into the reasons why you might be see-sawing between drinking and not-drinking. Through reflecting and analysing your personal feelings, you'll be better able to move on from ambivalence.

Lesson 7: It's not a slip up, it's a learning experience: Changing your relationship with alcohol might not be a smooth process. But it's an addictive drug, so that's understandable. Be kind to yourself, learn from your experiences and take action for a better future.

Lesson 8: The four energies: Becoming alcohol-free will increase your energy levels in all aspects of your life. It's important to notice and appreciate these benefits, as it will act as fuel to encourage you to make further positive changes.

Lesson 9: Enjoying the freedom of control: Removing the alcohol gives you that control back - control over your response to life and control because alcohol no longer drives your thoughts.

Lesson 10: Climb your own mountain: If you make changes, whether large or small and keep moving in the right direction, you'll discover you are reaping the benefits of a sober life, and achieving more than you imagined yourself capable of.

So, what's the big deal?

If you have absorbed all the Lessons up to now, hopefully you are pondering the same thing? What is alcohol actually the solution for? Or is removing it actually ....

" the world's best kept secret"

If I could know then what I know now I wouldn't have been fearful, sceptical, in denial.

If I could know then what I know now I would have been desperate to get going, eager to try out this new life.

So often we are encouraged by the media to try something that will change our lives, to buy products that will elevate us, enhance us in some way. We are encouraged to expect more out of life. We sign up to new hobbies, crazes, lifestyle changes without hesitation, but have we ignored the one thing that would win over everything else because it is tucked away, disguised as something else?

Removing alcohol is the gift that keeps on giving, and as I said at the beginning, I believe the person without alcohol is.....

Authentically me

I wasn't prepared for it. I hadn't expected to feel so different, to want to change so many elements of my life, to expand my mind trying new things and exploring new ideas. I hadn't realised I would feel so much calmer or when the "stressed" or "sad" me still comes out, that I would recover so much quicker. When you discover the authenticity behind the alcohol mask you too might find you invite more in, both people and experiences. You invite in more life.

Authentically you

You may not be there yet and that's okay. You may not know where "there" is at this moment and that's okay too. My book introduces a new perspective, gives you the lessons to enable you to try out The Sober Experience and an open invitation to repeat elements of the process as you need.

I hope you now believe me when I say that giving up alcohol is one action, but the ripple effect is infinite. When you are ready, it is what you make it. The energy levels will increase, the fog will lift, life will challenge you but you will cope better without alcohol. Life will change but you will find alternative paths more easily with clarity of mind. So what are you waiting for?

***

"Sometimes when you're in a dark place you think you've been buried, but you've actually been planted."

Christine Caine

References

Unless indicated, all definitions cited in my book are from the Cambridge dictionary

MY STORY

(1)The Minnesota Model in the Management of Drug and Alcohol Dependency: miracle, method or myth? Part II CHRISTOPHER C. H. COOK, B.Sc, M.R.C. This model was developed by two men in the 1950s who were working at a state mental hospital in Minnesota. The treatment combined professional and non-professional (recovering) support. The follow up studies were limited and a study in the 1980s where a small cohort were followed up after a year of leaving the facility found only 46% were abstinent. 28 days as a form of recovery can't be looked at in isolation as this model from which the time line derived contained number of arms of support surrounding the abstinence. https://onlinelibrary.wiley.com/

PART I

Why do we drink

(1) The pleasure pain principle - developed by Sigmund Freud to explain how the ID - the primitive and instinctual part of the mind drives behav-

iour. The ID could be compared to your chimp - that impulsive part of you that doesn't think before it acts.

(2) Alcohol Use Disorder - a term that was introduced in 2013 to combine the terms "alcohol abuse" and "alcohol dependence" a pattern of drinking that causes health problems or distress (NHS). AUD can be categorised as mild, moderate, or severe. It is a spectrum with alcoholism sitting at the far end, and anything over the recommended unit intake sitting at the lower end. So it acknowledges all drinkers that consume over recommended limits.

PART II

(1) The Monkey Mind - taken from The Chimp Paradox by Professor Steven Peters

(2) Internal Family Systems - by Dr Richard C. Schwartz, Ph.D.

(3) The Cycle of Change - created by James Prochaska and Carlo Di-Clemente, Ph.D. Originally called the Transtheoretical Model.

(4) The Growth Mindset - concept created by Carol S. Dweck, PhD

Potential blocks

(5) Loss aversion - a theory developed by Daniel Kahneman and Amos Tversky. It is a cognitive bias that causes people to prioritise avoiding losses over earning gains. Behavioural scientists believe that the pain of loss is felt more strongly than the pleasure of gain. - The decision lab - https://thedecisionlab.com

PART III

Lesson 1 the brain

(1) Information on blackouts taken from: National Institute on Alcohol Abuse and alcoholism www.niaaa.gov. Interrupted Memories: Alcohol Induced blackouts.

PART IV

Lesson 8

(1) The concept of the 4 dimension of energy: Physical, Emotional, Mental and spiritual was created by Dr Jim Loehr

(2) The Miracle Morning by Hal Elrod

APPENDIX I
Alcohol information

The physical impact alcohol will have on your body

Short term

- A hangover occurs when all the alcohol has left your system, when your blood alcohol concentration is zero - so you will wake up the next morning and it will hit you. The main symptoms.

- Tiredness - alcohol affects your sleep

- Nausea - the toxins moving around your body combine with acids in your stomach, and this is all churning around inside your body

- Memory problems - too much alcohol prevents your memories converting to short term, but in the hangover state too this problem continues

- Headache - dehydration, congeners in certain drinks, chemicals in your brain adjusting from withdrawal, other unknown factors as hangovers are still somewhat a mystery

- Hangxiety - the happy hormones that were boosted the night before are depleted the next day because the body is trying to balance itself, and tries to remove the excess hormones so you actually have less than normal

- Stress - drinking and being hungover cause a spike in the stress hormone Cortisol which affects our mental state and how we deal with daily life

- Immune system - a binge drinking session disrupts the immune system making you more weakened to fighting off infection

Long term

The long term effects off excessive drinking are extensive and I only bullet point some of them here.

- High blood pressure

- Liver disease

- Kidney damage

- Increased risk of gastrointestinal cancers

- Memory loss

- Nervous tissue damage

Withdrawal symptoms

When you stop drinking the body has to adjust from the removal of alcohol, and your body starts working harder to heal and recover and adapt to this new normal.

Secondly, there is a decreased responsiveness of GABA receptors in the brain. Remember we looked at those in the Brain chapter. It was the increase in this inhibitory neurotransmitter when we drink that causes that relaxed feeling. When we withdraw the alcohol it takes a while for the brain to catch up. Whilst we are drinking, the brain is trying to compensate for the increase in GABA by reducing the number of GABA receptors . When we remove alcohol this prevention process doesn't stop immediately, so it essentially causes the brain to be wired for a time as it isn't receiving the slowing down effect of alcohol.

A number of symptoms result from these two factors:

- Insomnia (difficulty sleeping)

- Tiredness or sobriety fatigue: your body is adjusting to a lot of changes so it is trying to rebalance

- Irritability

- Restlessness

- Anxiety

- Brain fog

- Hand tremors ('the shakes')

- Sweating

- A pulse rate above 100 beats per minute

- Nausea and vomiting

- Headaches

- Loss of appetite

- Depression

Withdrawal symptoms can be physical and psychological, and range in severity from mild to severe.

Milder symptoms usually start within 8 to 24 hours from the last alcoholic drink.

Severe symptoms can additionally include hallucinations (seeing, hearing, or feeling things that aren't real),4 as well as seizures or delirium tremens ('DTs').

WARNING - Delirium tremens

Heavy drinkers who suddenly decrease or stop drinking altogether may experience severe withdrawal symptoms. They are potentially dangerous. Approximately 1 in 10 people with alcohol withdrawal syndrome are affected by seizures. If left untreated, up to one in three of these patients go on to experience delirium tremens. Delirium tremens is a severe indication of alcohol withdrawal. Symptoms include:

□□Severe disorientation/hallucinations

□□Increased heart rate, blood pressure and breathing problems

□□ Uncontrollable restless behaviour

□□Severe agitation

These severe withdrawal effects normally occur three days into withdrawal and can last for two or three days and can be life threatening.

Detox timeline

The first 24 hours - you might experience mild anxiety as your brain continues to reduce the GABA receptors, so your brain will be agitated and this might also cause a headache.

36 hours - you might experience low feelings as the happy hormones are stabilising. You might feel sick as your body works hard to cope with the new change.

2-3 days - this is when withdrawal will feel the worst.

Up to a week - slowly these symptoms lesson and disappear.

2 weeks plus - withdrawal from alcohol is physically draining. So, it will make you feel tired. When the physical symptoms subside, you will start to notice the non-physical symptoms more. This can often be when you are tempted to drink again, so look out for this. As we discussed in the Mind chapter when some distance starts to grow from the pain of a hangover you might be tempted.

Genetics and alcohol use disorder

My parents were alcoholics. I don't know the history of those above them in the family tree as we weren't a close family. I had the fear that alcoholism was hereditary from a young age. I would so often hear people say that it was, but I didn't want to consider that it would be a problem for me. I didn't want to consider that I perhaps shouldn't drink. As time went on and I embarked on my drinking career, the fear subsided.

I won't go into detail about the genetics, as I am not qualified to do so, but I will explain a couple of facts around family history and genetics.

There is an increased risk of being predisposed to alcohol use disorder if there is a family history.

There is no alcoholism gene as such, but there are a number of genres that affect the risk of alcoholism. For example, there are two genes that relate to how alcohol is metabolised, ADH1B and ALDH2. These genes have the strongest known effects on risk for alcoholism. Studies have also identified other genes which increase the risk of alcoholism, but studies are ongoing.

Further information can be found at:- https://pmc.ncbi.nlm.nih.gov/art icles/PMC4056340/.

As someone who has lived through parental alcoholism, who has seen the link with mental health problems in my mother, who has seen the impact of environmental (specifically financial and family breakdown) in my mother, as someone who feels they have been most directly impacted by societal pressure and childhood trauma over any hereditary links, I would say having an awareness of the possible risks is useful but knowing that it is by no means a conclusive link was an important learning. For me, acknowledging the other factors and influences was more beneficial. This knowledge gave me the power to make the necessary changes and stick with them.

Research shows that many factors contribute to Alcohol Use Disorder, not just any potential biological links. But for me, knowing there might be a genetic link encouraged me to have complete abstinence. It drives my sobriety rather than pushes me to what could be perceived by some as an inevitable drink problem.

So, as I have mentioned above, and supporting this through lived experience, genetics is definitely only one factor that might contribute to developing Alcohol Use Disorder. Environmental, social, and cultural factors, past trauma, the age that you start at, other mental health problems - all of these have a potential impact. What we have tackled in this book are the factors that drive the mind's response to alcohol, but for completeness I acknowledge the genetic component. For me, any concerns in this area would be a key reason to make complete abstinence the end goal, rather than simply reduce the volume that you drink.

Units of alcohol

Understanding the concept of units of alcohol is helpful when it comes to understanding how long our bodies take to process alcohol. This then provides some explanation as to how the neurotransmitters are impacting our brain at different stages of the evening as they respond to increasing levels of alcohol consumption.

- One unit of alcohol is the equivalent to half a glass of wine, half a regular strength beer or a small measure of spirits

- It takes the body roughly one hour to metabolise a unit of alcohol

- Alcohol goes straight to your bloodstream and is then dispersed throughout your body meaning you feel the effects pretty rapidly - within around 10 minutes depending on the strength of the alcohol

- The UK guidelines state that safe drinking limits are 14 units a week spread over three days or more

The more you drink on a regular basis, the more you're likely to be affected by withdrawal symptoms.

Alcohol unit reference

Avenues of support

In the UK, the Government website will provide you with a list of services in your area. Please go to the following link for support.

https://www.nhs.uk/nhs-services/find-alcohol-addiction-support-services/

There are also a number of alcohol charities that have a huge amount of information and support:

www.drinkaware.co.uk This charity works with individuals, with the Government and within the community

www.mind.org.uk - as an alternative to the government website Mind lists a number of support avenues that can be taken

www.nacoa.org.uk - helps individuals who are affected by their parents drinking

APPENDIX II
Additional Information on my website

If you connect with my website you will find a resources page with additional information to support you in this Sober Experience

www.thesoberexperience.co.uk/resources

Books: These books really changed my perspective on life, they gave me a new focus when I stopped drinking and they made me stronger. Everyone follows their own path, but if you want a few insights on my path then take a look.

Audios: I have created some audios for those trigger moments. They are short audios to support you in the moment.

Templates: There are some useful templates to support positive change on my website, such as journaling, monthly goal setting and positivity tracker.

Courses and webinars: I periodically run courses and webinars to support the lessons in the book. So sign up for information on my website.

More from the author

Samantha Roome is a Sober coach with an ICF-accredited diploma in Positive Psychology and Alcohol-Free coaching. She was inspired to retrain and diversify from her 20 year Finance career in 2020 when she stopped drinking herself. With her mission to normalise the conversation around alcohol she runs alcohol support programs and supports local sober groups and drug and alcohol charities. She is also a mum to three children, one with a rare chromosome disorder and autism so is passionate about sharing how powerful navigating parenthood (and additional needs parenthood) sober can be.

Books

The Ten Lessons will be released later in the new year as part of The Sober Experience series. This second book purely focuses in on the ten lessons but in more detail to give you the reinforcement and a resource to quickly refer to.

Speaking

Sam brings the essence of her book and her program along with some key messages, tips and guidance in an accessible format to allow businesses to bring the topic of alcohol into their organisation and to allow us all to "normalise the conversation around alcohol."

Groups

At the time of writing Sam has created a Facebook group around the Sober Experience. Please join for that extra support and connection.

https://www.facebook.com/groups/thesoberexperience

www.ingramcontent.com/pod-product-compliance
Lightning Source LLC
Chambersburg PA
CBHW031132090426
42738CB00008B/1056